"NOW CHOOSE LIFE"

Conversion as the Way to Life

William A. Barry, S.J.

Paulist Press
New York Mahwah

Imprimi Potest
Very Rev. Robert E. Manning, S.J., Provincial
Society of Jesus of New England

Library of Congress Cataloging-in-Publication Data

Barry, William A.
    Now choose life: conversion as the way to life/by William
A. Barry
        p. cm.
    Includes bibliographical references.
    ISBN 0-8091-3230-3
    1. Conversion.   2. Christian life—Catholic authors.   I. Title.
BV4916.B326   1990
248.2′4—dc20   90-20918
                                                                   CIP

Published by Paulist Press
997 Macarthur Boulevard
Mahwah, New Jersey 07430

Printed and bound in the
United States of America

Table of Contents

To the May Family
My Sister Kathleen and Her Late Husband Bert
and Their Children
Mary Beth Knoeppel, Bill, Mike,
Stephen, Helene and Matt
With Love and Gratitude for Your Love

Foreword

This little book treats conversion as a gift of God drawing us progressively away from illusion into the reality of the created universe and of God. I am deeply grateful to Don Brophy of Paulist Press who asked me to do it and put so much faith in my ability to pull it off. I hope that it will be helpful to many people who desire to know and love God with all their hearts and with all their minds and with all their strength and their neighbor as themselves. The desire is itself God's gift in creating us. I hope that the book will also be taken as a paean of gratitude to God, Father, Son and Holy Spirit, whose creative love makes it possible for us not only to desire union with God but to hope to attain it.

Besides my gratitude to Don Brophy, I am also grateful to my family, to my father who still reads whatever I write, to my sisters Peg and Mary who so generously read and so enthusiastically commented on the manuscript, and to the May family to whom I have dedicated this book. (*Finally,* say my nieces and nephews.) I have some wonderful friends who continually encourage me in my writing and who read manuscripts without a whimper. So I thank Philomena Sheerin and Mary Guy, not only for their support but especially for their friendship. Five friends were particularly helpful in reading the first draft of this manuscript in a hurry and giving me detailed and very useful feedback: Marika Geoghegan, Paul Lucey, S.J., Ellen Nelson, R.S.C.J., Myles Sheehan, S.J. and Chris Rupert, S.J. The latter spent two extra days at Boston College just to read the manuscript, and went over it in great and loving detail. Marika Geoghegan was especially helpful in giving me a feminist's perspective on the first draft. I am profoundly thankful to the five of them.

During the writing of this book I have been the rector of the Jesuit Community at Boston College. The community has been enormously supportive of me both in encouraging me in writing and in caring for me. Two members of the community, Harvey D. Egan, S.J., and Joseph D. Gauthier, S.J., not only encouraged me to accept the offer to write the book, but also helped me to begin thinking creatively about how to go about it. I am very grateful to them. I could not have written anything during my tenure as rector without the support of the staff of the Jesuit Community who do most of the work that makes our community such a happy place. I want to thank Lawrence Foley, S.J., Joseph Killilea, Paul Nash, S.J. and Francis Venuta, S.J. I owe a special debt of gratitude to the community secretary, Cyrilla Mooradian and to the administrator of the community, James M. Collins, S.J., without whom I would be lost. The many men and women who see me for spiritual direction have enriched my knowledge of God by trusting me with their experiences. I am grateful to all of them, and especially to those who have given me permission to cite their experiences (without, of course, divulging their identity). Thanks is a small word to carry all that is in my heart for all these friends and the many others who have made this little book possible, but it is the only one I have. Thanks!

1

What Do We Really Want?

Freud once made the remark that, despite all his research and reflection, he could not answer the question, "What do women want?" No doubt, a male chau-
vinistic remark, but also, because prejudiced, terribly
shortsighted and narrow-minded. The fact is that the
deepest question facing any study of human beings,
male or female, is: "What do we really want?" And we
have a forest full of answers to that question.

The popularity of state-run lotteries in the United
States and other countries gives the impression that
many people want money, or at least what money can
buy. Some want security for a rainy day. Some want to
be able to afford a suitable home. Some want to be able
to provide more for their children and grandchildren.
Some dream of the exotic vacation or the luxuries they
might have if they hit the jackpot. Many must dream of
living the lives of the rich and famous and perhaps of
hobnobbing with them. Witness in the past few years
the ratings of such soap opera shows as "Dallas," "Dy-
nasty" and "Knots Landing."

Like many persons Hannah, in the First Book of
Samuel, wanted a child. People desire posterity for many
reasons. Hannah was embittered by the treatment she
received from her husband Elkanah's other wife who
flaunted her children before the childless Hannah. For
some people children seem to give assurance of being

cared for in old age. For others children promise that one's name will live on in memory even after one's death. Many couples, of course, desire to bring new life into the world as a sign of their love for one another and because life has, for all its difficulties, been good to them. Many people seem to be obsessed with the desire to be revenged. In the *Aeneid* Dido, the jilted queen of Carthage, wishes that posterity will arise as her avenger against Aeneas and his posterity. One of the most poignant and beautiful psalms of the Bible ends with these terrible words of vengeance:

> O Daughter of Babylon, doomed to destruction,
> happy is he who repays you
> for what you have done to us—
> he who seizes your infants
> and dashes them against the rocks (Ps 137:8–9).

In our own day we have seen the terrible desire for vengeance that consumes people with hatred for their "enemies" and draws people to the sites of executions of criminals to cheer when the lights dim as the electric chair is activated.

Obviously people crave security against enemies or perceived enemies. The superpowers have very nearly bankrupted themselves building more and more weapons of mass destruction, and most of their citizens have applauded the leaders who have been the instruments of this mad arms race. The one thing every presidential candidate in the United States since the end of World War II has had to prove was that he was not soft on communism. The madness of it all shows itself in the fact that we have not bought security. Terror seems to be on the rise in our world.

It is clear from the advertising industry, if from nothing else, that many people desire to look beautiful and attractive to the opposite sex. Obviously sex sells products. The desire for sexual fulfillment exerts a very strong pull on human beings.

The great achievements of science could only be possible because of the deep desire of scientists for knowledge of how the universe works. Indeed, this desire for knowledge fuels the amazing development of babies and children. Some educators, in fact, attribute at least part of the failure of schools to achieve more than they do to their inability or unwillingness to capitalize on the innate wonder in children. Obviously, too, we desire beauty both to admire it in the wondrous beauty of our natural world and to create it in works of art. Many people center their lives on the pursuit of knowledge or the pursuit of beauty.

Clearly, then, Freud's complaint was one-sided; it is not easy to know what men as well as women want. As we begin this study of the theme of conversion, it seems very appropriate to try to answer this crucial question the best way we can. There must be some deeper desire than all these somewhat superficial desires that drives the human heart. To begin to answer the question, "What do we most deeply desire?" let us look at the first chapters of the book of Genesis with the hope that we will there discover our deepest desire.

The first chapter of Genesis contains one tradition of the creation story. When I hear the story read at the Easter Vigil liturgy, my heart swells at the crescendo of the days of creation. Each day ends with God's sigh of contentment, "And God saw that it was good." The crescendo ends with these words of God:

> Let us make man in our image, in our likeness, and let them rule over the fish of the sea and the birds of the air, over the livestock, over all the earth, and over all the creatures that move along the ground.
> So God created man in his image, in the image of God he created him; male and female he created them.

Finally, "God saw all that he had made, and it was very good. And there was evening, and there was morning— the sixth day."

The text seems to go out of its way to stress the goodness of the universe as it comes from the creative hand of God. The universe really is "original blessing," to use the title of one of Matthew Fox's books. The universe is the apple of God's eye. The Book of Wisdom catches the mood in a lovely poem:

> The whole world, for you, can no more than
> tip a balance,
> like a drop of morning dew falling on the
> ground.
> Yet you are merciful to all, because you are
> almighty,
> you overlook people's sins, so that they can
> repent.
> Yes, you love everything that exists,
> and nothing that you have made disgusts you,
> since, if you had hated something, you would
> not have made it.

And how could a thing subsist, had you not
    willed it?
Or how be preserved, if not called forth by you?
No, you spare all, since all is yours, Lord, lover
    of life! (Wis 11:22–26. *New Jersualem
    Bible.*)

The mood of creative love in Genesis continues
with the introduction of another tradition of creation in
chapter 2. God creates the Garden of Eden into which
God introduces the first human being, called the man
(*Adam*). Once again we hear the compassion and kindness of God in the words, "It is not good for the man to
be alone. I will make a helper suitable for him." No
other creature is found suitable for the man until God
formed the woman in whom the man rejoiced. This
chapter also ends on a positive note. "The man and his
wife were both naked, and they felt no shame." Moreover, we get the impression from a remark in chapter 3
that God and the man and the woman had a habit of
walking together in the Garden of Eden in the cool of the
day and that the human beings were not ashamed of
their nakedness.

These stories of the creation of the universe speak
to our hearts, our desires, do they not? What do we really
want? We want to live without shame or fear of who we
are. We want to live in a universe in which we are in
harmony with all of creation, especially with all human
beings and even more especially with the Mystery at the
heart of the universe, the Creator who is "lover of life."

C. S. Lewis found himself repeatedly "surprised by
Joy," a desire for he knew not what, but which he eventually recognized as God. In the preface to the third edi-
tion of *The Pilgrim's Regress: An Allegorical Apology*

for Christianity, Reason and Romanticism, Lewis describes the experience of this Joy as "one of intense longing" which is distinguished from other longings by two things. "In the first place, though the sense of want is acute and even painful, yet the mere wanting is felt to be somehow a delight." The paradox is that even though this desire is not satisfied, the desire itself is better than the satisfaction of any other longing. "This hunger is better than any other fullness; this poverty better than all other wealth." Secondly, we can easily be mistaken about the object of the desire. In fact, Lewis makes clear, for most of his life until his conversion to Christianity he tried to satisfy this desire with objects that did not satisfy and could not satisfy the desire. He concludes:

> It appeared to me therefore that if a man diligently followed this desire, pursuing the false objects until their falsity appeared and then resolutely abandoning them, he must come out at last into the clear knowledge that the human soul was made to enjoy some object that is never fully given—nay, cannot even be imagined as given—in our present mode of subjective and spatio-temporal experience (pp. 7–10).

So the deepest desire of the human heart is for the Mystery we call God. Augustine put it in a pithy aphorism. "You have made us for yourself, and our hearts are restless until they rest in you." The whole of his *Confessions* can be seen as a paean to that desire and a painful confession of how he, like C. S. Lewis centuries later, kept turning away from the real object of that desire.

If we take the mythic visions of Genesis seriously, we will come to the conclusion that God creates a universe where all persons are called to live in harmony and in community with God and one another. That creative touch of God is the heart of creation. All of creation yearns for the fulfillment God intended for it. The Garden of Eden is, therefore, the mythic vision, not so much of the first moment of creation, but of creation's fulfillment.

The late Scottish philosopher John Macmurray concludes that the universe is one action of God. As one action it is governed by one intention which we can only come to know if God chooses to reveal it to us. Jesus, Christians believe, is the ultimate, unique revelation of God's intention. He reveals that God is self-sacrificing love, that nothing we do, no matter how heinous, will change God from the Mysterious One who both loves us into existence and continually draws us by his love to enter into community with God. Paul tried to express this revelation in a number of places in his letters. In Ephesians we read:

> Praise be to the God and Father of our Lord Jesus Christ, who has blessed us in the heavenly realms with every spiritual blessing in Christ. For he chose us in him before the creation of the world to be holy and blameless in his sight. In love he predestined us to be adopted as his sons and daughters through Jesus Christ, in accordance with his pleasure and will. . . . And he made known to us the mystery of his will according to his good pleasure, which he purposed in Christ, to be put into effect when the times will have reached their fulfillment—to bring all things in heaven and on earth together under one head, even Christ (Eph 1:3–10).

And in Romans Paul seems to pick up on the yearning at the heart of the creation:

> We know that the whole creation has been groaning as in the pains of childbirth right up to the present time. Not only so, but we ourselves, who have the firstfruits of the Spirit, groan inwardly as we wait eagerly for our adoption as sons and daughters, the redemption of our bodies. For in this hope we were saved. But hope that is seen is no hope at all. Who hopes for what he already has? But if we hope for what we do not yet have, we wait for it patiently.
>
> In the same way, the Spirit helps us in our weakness. We do not know what we ought to pray for, but the Spirit himself intercedes for us with groans that words cannot express. And he who searches our hearts knows the mind of the Spirit, because the Spirit intercedes for the saints in accordance with God's will (Rom 8:22–27).

God, it seems, wants the world to be a Garden of Eden where all people live in harmony not only with God, but also with one another and with the whole of the created order. That desire or intention or dream of God in a real sense powers the universe. Love is the deepest yearning of the whole of creation. This is the reality of the universe we inhabit.

Is it not the deepest desire of our hearts to live out this dream, this intention of God? Do not our hearts burn within us when we let ourselves tap into this dream? Precisely because this dream is the deepest desire of our hearts, they are lifted up when we hear the prophecies of the Hebrew Bible in Advent. We yearn for the day when "the wolf will live with the lamb," when "the infant will play near the hole of the cobra," when "(t)hey will neither harm nor destroy on all my holy mountain" (Is 11:6–9). We want to live in a universe where love, not fear and hatred, is dominant. In other words, we want what God wants for us and for our universe. And this desire is not for a pipe dream. It is a desire to live in tune with the deepest reality of our universe. In *Addiction and Grace* Gerald May writes:

> God creates us out of love . . . Scripture proclaims that this love, from which and for which we are created, is perfect. I do not presume to fully understand what this perfect love means, but I am certain that it draws us toward itself by means of our own deepest desires (p. 13).

These words remind us of what Lewis says of Joy, the desire for we know not what; namely, that it is the deepest longing of our hearts and that if we follow it resolutely, even when it latches on to objects that turn out to be idols, we will ultimately discover that the longing is for the Mystery we call God.

But, as Lewis indicates, we will have to recognize the idols we worship instead of God. For this we will need discernment, the kind of wisdom that can notice our reactions in this world and decide which of these reactions are leading us to the desire of the everlasting hills, and which are leading us up a garden path.

In the course of this book we will try to follow the path of this desire for the fullness of reality. The one thing we know with certainty is that we do not live in a world where this desire motivates much of our behavior, or the behavior of others, or of our institutions. If we are to let our lives be governed by this deepest desire of our hearts, and thus be in tune with God's desire for us and our universe, we need to "repent and believe the good news" (Mk 1:15). In other words, we need to be converted. I will maintain that this conversion of our hearts and minds means a conversion from illusion to more and more realism. What looks like "pie in the sky" idealism will have to be seen as the most down-to-earth realism. The "good news" Jesus preached is about reality, not about idealism.

In both the Old and New Testaments the two words for conversion refer to a radical redirection of one's life. One word (*nacham* in Hebrew and *metanoia* in Greek) refers to a turning away from something; the other (*shub* and *epistrophe*) refers to a turning toward something. Usually the understanding is that one turns away from sin and toward God. In the course of this book we will see that conversion means turning away from illusion and toward reality. The "good news" is that the deepest reality of our world is God, the Trinity of Persons, who invites all of us to live in community with God and all persons and in harmony with the universe. But it is "good news" that is strangely difficult for us to believe.

2

Is Hope for a Just
and Harmonious World
a Delusion?

Social scientists have described an hypothesis by which many people ward off anxiety about life on this planet: the "just world hypothesis." When people read of the rape of a woman, the just world hypothesis is invoked to ward off anxiety about their own vulnerability if they say to themselves, "She must have taken a chance by walking in the wrong area." In other words, if something unjust happens, the tendency is to explain it away, and one way is to blame the victim. The friends of Job who try by all kinds of arguments to convince him that he must have merited his troubles are using the "just world hypothesis." When six Jesuit priests and their cook and her daughter were brutally slain by the military in El Salvador in November, 1989, at least some people believed that they were killed because they were Communists and in league with the Communist revolutionaries. When we hear of a man who has contracted cancer, we almost instinctively wonder whether he smoked cigarettes or ate the wrong foods. We could go on with examples. The point of the hypothesis is that it gives us the illusion that life is in our control, that we can control our fate. If crippling illness can strike out of the blue, then I am vulnerable. If I can find a reason that justifies someone else's bad fortune, then it is not "bad fortune," but "just," and I can go on believing that I am in control of my destiny. The world is not always a just place, obviously. Not only is it not just in the way this subconscious hypothesis uses it to stave off anxiety, but even more fundamentally our world is not just or harmonious. Bad news seems to be the rule not the exception. Millions of men, women and children have been killed in wars and famines in this century alone. Innocent civilians are killed by terrorist bombings. All over the world prisoners of conscience are tortured and killed unjustly. The goods of this world are not distributed in any way that even approaches fairness. The resources of the world's poorest nations are plundered by the wealthier nations. Afro-American and Latino-American children in the United States are raised in conditions that breed cycles of poverty. Women are paid consistently below the scale of men for comparable work. We live in a world where technological advances promise the means to feed, clothe, shelter and educate billions of human beings, to provide health care for everyone, and to make it possible for all who want to to live meaningful lives. Yet, according to Joseph de Rivera, the governments of the world spend $17 billion dollars every two weeks on military expenditures and thus drain off the resources that could be used for a more just world. Most of us feel helpless to do anything about the injustices that surround us. In almost a despairing way we remind ourselves of Jesus' saying, "You will always have the poor among you" (Jn 12:8), shrug and figure that not only is the belief in a just world a delusion but so is the hope that one can come about. Are we correct? Or do we need to be converted in this area?

In a remarkable article in *Social Justice Research,* Joseph de Rivera, professor of psychology at Clark University, argues that for its own survival the world needs new people. He maintains that the kind of self-image people now have is the product of our culture and upbringing and, with John Macmurray, he holds that the image of the "self" is developed by different cultures as a strategy for dealing with an inhospitable world.

Macmurray postulates that human beings are moved to action by two fundamental motives: love for the other and fear for oneself. A third motive, hatred, is derived from fear, but need not concern us here. Love for the other is the motive that moves us to care for the other, to look for the other's good. When this motive is dominant in us, we move out toward the other, we act with trust and hope in the world. When fear predominates, we withdraw into ourselves to protect ourselves. There are two basic strategies for dealing with predominant fear: an aggressive one and a conforming one. The aggressive stance leads to the autonomous, self-sufficient and self-interested individual and to a society where the self-interests of individuals need to be governed by law so that there is at least some justice. Rivera notes that this strategy is the one generally adopted by Western civilization. Psychological literature often sees this as the strategy of the stereotypical male. The conformist stance leads to the submissive, group-oriented self and to a society where behavior is governed by conventions. Rivera shows that Eastern civilizations generally foster this strategy. Psychology tends to see this as the strategy of the stereotypical female. Neither of these strategies leads to a world where genuine community is possible since the predominant motive is fear, fear for oneself and fear for one's way of life. Since this way of life is seen as necessary to deal with an inhospitable world, it must be protected at all costs. Moreover, neither of these strategies satisfies the deepest desire of our hearts, which, as we have seen, is to live in harmony and community with all people. Rivera, therefore, proposes a new model of the self, one in which love for the other is the predominant motive for action and community the real hope.

What are the characteristics of such a self? Rivera describes the person in seven points. I summarize here those which are relevant to our purposes: 1. With care for the other as my main motive I can cooperate with others, not just to meet my individual needs nor to be accepted by the others, but in mutuality. The unit of the personal is not the individual "I," but "I and Thou." 2. Because fear is subordinated to love, I am less defensive and can pay attention to and understand others and their viewpoints as well as express my own opinions with relative unambiguity. 3. With the motive of love dominant my caring for others is more important than concern for myself. Hence, I help others to develop without imposing myself on them. 4. I can enter into open and honest negotiations with others over conflicting positions because I care for them more than I fear for myself and for my concerns. In fact, "we" are more important than my own concerns. As a result it is easier honestly to forgive others for offenses. This portrait of the "new person" which Rivera believes the world needs for its own survival looks remarkably like the portrait of the kind of person God wants as the fulfillment of God's dream.

This "new person" is not without fears. First, there

are realistic fears. I can love someone who menaces me, and at the same time fear the menace. Rivera puts it this way: "The model simply calls for fear to be subordinated to care so that as one copes with sociopaths, cheaters, unjust power, cynicism and apathy one is not so overwhelmed that one becomes primarily concerned with oneself." In addition, care for the other does not mean losing oneself in dependence on the other for all one's sense of self-worth. Moreover, the model does not expect that the "new person" will be able to maintain the caring stance all the time. If, however, I have once experienced for some time the subordination of fear to love, then I can, Rivera maintains, return to wholeness when fear has become dominant. Here is where Rivera and I may part company, but I will take that point up shortly.

Rivera believes that we need to bend every effort to help people and, through them, societies to subordinate fear to love. If more and more people not only imagine a world where community reigns but also act to bring it about, a more just world will eventuate. Is he, too, just a pipe dreamer? Rather than concentrate on bad news, which is all around us, he points to research and experience that indicates that there are people who are already acting in a caring, mutual way even outside of the family context. After noting how many people do not participate in the political process, even in a democracy, he points out that a surprisingly large number of people do, and apparently with the motive of disinterested care. The civil rights movement in the fifties and sixties is one noteworthy example. Bread for the World has 40,000 members who lobby the American Congress for the poor and hungry of this world. The recent peaceful revolutions in the Philippines and in Czechoslovakia required that many ordinary people subordinate their fears for themselves to their care for one another and put their bodies on the line. Gandhi was able to mobilize masses of Indians to demonstrate nonviolently and to maintain the attitude of care for the British whom they resisted. In other words, there are examples of people who have acted out of the motive of care, and they have achieved results. As a result of their efforts, a little bit of the world was, for at least some time, more just.

The "basic Christian communities" of South America provide another example. A few years ago I lived for about a week in a "favela" in Sao Paulo, Brazil. The favela was a section of the periphery of Sao Paulo where people had begun to build homes as squatters. The homes were in all stages of development, from makeshift shanties to cinder block houses. Some houses had running water and electricity, but many, if not most, did not. Drinking water came from a few standpipes, and many people washed their clothes and themselves in a dirty little stream that ran through the favela. The people were dirt poor and had to travel miles on very poor public transportation to get what work they could. Here, if anywhere, one would expect to find love subordinated to fear. Yet, although it was by no means a perfect community, people did care for one another. They watched out for one another. They had set up a day care center and were trying to provide schooling for their children. The most impressive of their cooperative efforts was the little church they were in the process of building together. In their spare time they had gathered cinder blocks and put up the walls. Just before I arrived, they had been able to lay down cement on the dirt floor. There were no proper windows or door yet, but it was their house of worship and meeting. Moreover, at the liturgy I celebrated in my halting Portuguese they expressed themselves openly and honestly and hopefully during the shared homily. These people, in spite of extremely difficult circumstances, retained their hope for a more just world and the belief that they could do something together to make their part of it a little more just. Rivera describes the ordeal of Aldolpho Pérez Esquivel, the 1980 winner of the Nobel Peace Prize. He has committed himself to working to help the poor by nonviolent means. During Argentina's military regime he was imprisoned and tortured. In spite of the fearful ordeal he was not dominated by fear or hatred, nor, according to Rivera who met him, did the ordeal leave him with psychic scars. "Instead," says Rivera, "I found the most open person I have ever had the privilege of meeting, a man who was incredibly powerful because of his capacity for vulnerability." Rivera notes that Esquivel speaks of prayer and faith as what sustained him. Here, of course, the psychologist as such cannot comprehend what has happened, and Rivera acknowledges this fact. But I wonder whether anyone can live, for long, a life where fear is subordinated to love without some turn to a "higher power"; without prayer, in other words. Earlier I noted that Rivera and I may diverge on the point of whether by willpower alone people can return themselves to the standpoint of subordinating fear to love when they have fallen into the dominance of fear. There is a danger in thinking that it can be done by one's own power. Trying hard or harder to overcome one's fears, I have noticed, has usually led to more self-absorption and to frustration and depression. Esquivel attributes his attitude to faith and prayer. Only thus could he forgive those who had tortured him. Perhaps, too, only by this faith could he be saved from the self-righteousness that can come if one believes that one has triumphed by one's own right hand.

Another example that indicates that the attitude of care for one's "enemies" is really possible and makes life not only bearable but even happy in spite of hellish circumstances is provided by the Dutch Jewess, Etty Hillesum, who died in Auschwitz on November 30, 1943. In her diary, published under the title *An Interrupted Life: The Diaries of Etty Hillesum 1941–43,* she says, knowing full well that arrest and transport await her, "For once you have begun to walk with God, you need only keep on walking with Him and all of life becomes one long stroll—such a marvellous feeling. . . . I hate nobody. I am not embittered. And once the love of mankind has germinated in you, it will grow without measure" (p. 149). Her diary is a record of how she was transformed from a self-centered young woman into the kind of mystic who could write such lines in the hell that was occupied Amsterdam for Jews. The following paragraph was written after she saw more and more signs of the restrictions put on Jews by the Germans:

> But above the one narrow path still left to us stretches the sky, intact. They can't do anything to us, they really can't. They can harass us, they can rob us of our material goods, of our freedom of movement, but we ourselves forfeit our greatest assets by our misguided compliance. By our feelings of being persecuted, humiliated and oppressed. By our own hatred. . . . We may of course be sad and depressed by what has been done to us; that is only human and understandable. However: our greatest injury is one we inflict upon ourselves. I find life beautiful and I

feel free. The sky within me is as wide as the one stretching above my head. I believe in God and I believe in man and I say so without embarrassment. Life is hard, but that is no bad thing. . . . True peace will come only when every individual finds peace within himself; when we have all vanquished and transformed our hatred for our fellow human beings of whatever race—even into love one day, although perhaps that is asking too much. It is, however, the only solution. I am a happy person and I hold life dear indeed, in this year of Our Lord 1942, the umpteenth year of the war (p. 151).

Is the hope of a just world a delusion? It is if we believe it is. But then we will be part of the problem. We will be living in the illusory world where fear predominates and where people believe that they can conquer their fears either by aggressiveness or submission. We will not be living in the world of reality which is the world God is creating and in which the impulse to subordinate fear to love comes from the Holy Spirit who dwells in our hearts. Once again, it is a question of whether we will put our trust in the "thing with feathers," as Emily Dickinson defines hope, and beg God to convert our hearts so that fear is subordinate to love.

3

How Can Our Hearts Be Changed?

With Rivera we have concluded that our hearts need to be changed if we are to be able to attune ourselves to God's dream for our universe and our own deepest desires, and if our world is to become more just and harmonious. For the most part, our hearts are not centered on God nor do they subordinate fear for ourselves to love for others and God. The dominance of fear not only affects our relationships with God and other people but also affects intergroup and international relations and our relations with the environment. Our world, as we noted, is neither as just nor as harmonious as God desires it to be and as we ourselves desire it to be. How do we allow our hearts to be changed or converted?

One clue to an answer is provided by the words of C. S. Lewis cited in the first chapter. You recall that he had described Joy as the deepest desire of the human heart. That desire gets derailed from its real object to pursue false ones. But, he believes, if a person diligently followed this desire,

> . . . pursuing the false objects until their falsity
> appeared and then resolutely abandoning them,
> he must come out at last into the clear knowl-
> edge that the human soul was made to enjoy
> some object that is never fully given—nay, can-

not even be imagined as given—in our present mode of subjective and spatio-temporal experience.

In order to discover the falsity of these objects we need to develop the skill of discernment of spirits. I want to pursue this subject in this chapter, but will begin at some distance from it. I believe that our age is experiencing a spiritual crisis comparable, perhaps, to the spiritual crisis of Europe at the time of the Reformation as the medieval period gave way to the Renaissance. Our crisis, however, is worldwide.

In a remarkably prescient series of broadcast lectures on the BBC in 1930 and 1932, John Macmurray diagnosed the modern problem as the loss of faith (*Freedom in the Modern World*). When we lose faith, he argued, "we lose the power of action; we lose the capacity of choice, we lose our grip on reality and so our sanity." By "faith," he seems to mean, not an intellectual assent to truths, but a heartfelt commitment to transcendent values and to God's intention for our world. Apparently Paul also used the term "faith" in the same sense. In the *New Jerome Biblical Commentary* Joseph Fitzmyer notes that for Paul faith "is not a mere intellectual assent to the proposition that 'Jesus is Lord.' It is a vital, personal commitment, engaging the whole person to Christ in all his or her relations with God, other human beings, and the world" (p. 1407). By and large, Macmurray would say, the emotions and feelings, the hearts, in other words, of modern men and women are not centered in the God and Father of our Lord Jesus Christ. Hence our hearts are not centered in the real world God is continually creating, and so we face a deep crisis of faith.

Macmurray maintains that since the breakup of the medieval world Westerners have allowed their minds to develop in freedom. As a result we have seen a tremendous development of knowledge of which modern science and technology are a testimony. He believes, however, that:

> . . . there has been no corresponding emotional development. As a result we are intellectually civilized and emotionally primitive; and we have reached the point at which the development of knowledge threatens to destroy us. Knowledge is power, but emotion is the master of our values and of the uses, therefore, to which we put our power. Emotionally we are primitive, childish, undeveloped. Therefore, we have the tastes, the appetites, the interests and apprehensions of children. But we have in our hands a vast set of powers, which are the products of our intellectual development. We have used these powers to construct an intricate machinery of life, all in the service of our childish desires. And now we are waking up to the fact that we cannot control it; that we do not even know what we want to do with it. So we are beginning to be afraid of the work of our hands. That is the modern dilemma (pp. 47–48).

When Macmurray speaks of Westerners, he is thinking primarily, I believe, of European and North American men. Women, by and large, have not let their emotions remain undeveloped; moreover, women have, by and large, not been allowed to be shapers of Western culture, either religious or secular. In the rest of this analysis I will stress that Macmurray's analysis applies mostly to such men.

Macmurray believes that we Westerners have allowed our minds the freedom to seek the truth whereever it may be found, but we have not given our emotions, our affective lives a similar freedom. Indeed, men have tended to distrust and disparage emotions and affectivity. The mind is rational, emotions are irrational, men, at least, tend to believe. As a result of this distrust and the consequent underdevelopment of their affective lives Westerners as a whole have not internalized God's values. Thus, in Macmurray's eyes, they have lost faith. In 1930 Macmurray could only dimly intuit the horrors to which reliance on the "rationality" of our minds and obedience to authority might lead. We now know about the gulags, the concentration camps, the "final solution," the atomic and hydrogen bombs, the "killing fields," the "accidents" at Three Mile Island and at Chernobyl, the oil spill in Alaska, those triumphs of the intellect unbridled by a well-developed emotional life. Emotions are not the only aspects of human nature that can be irrational. These horrors of our modern world were the products of the minds of human beings, overwhelmingly men, with underdeveloped emotions and feelings and values.

Macmurray saw that we must cultivate our emotions or lose the very freedom of thought we prize so much.

We are standing, today, at the second crisis of our European history; the second great crisis in the fight for human freedom. The first was the crisis in which we chose, after much fear and hesitation and persecution, to trust one another to think for ourselves and to stand by the expression of our honest thought. Now we are called upon to implement that faith in the human mind by trusting in the integrity of human feeling (pp. 52–53).

Trust in our feelings does not mean, for Macmurray, to act on any feeling. Just as the mind had to discipline itself to seek the truth of the real world, so too we must "set out to discover, through feeling, the real values of our world and of our life in the world." In other words, our feelings must become attuned to reality just as our minds must. Macmurray echoes the prescription of C. S. Lewis when he says that "(w)e shall have to submit to the discipline of our feelings, not by authority nor by tradition, but by life itself." Submission to such discipline will not be "cheap grace," to use the phrase of Dietrich Bonhoeffer; it will not give us "security or pleasure or happiness or comfort, . . . but a slow, gradual realization of the goodness of the world and of living in it" (p. 53).

Macmurray maintains, therefore, that our emotions can become as rational, as attuned to reality, as our intellects. But such rationality is not obtained by fiat or by merely willing it or by blind obedience. We must allow our emotional life the freedom to find its own rationality through trial and error, through the disciplined willingness to feel what we feel and to test those feelings against reality. It can seem that Macmurray is arguing for untrammeled freedom to act on one's feelings and desires. Not so. For him the reality against which one must test one's feelings is the real world which is God's world governed by God's one intention. Macmurray claims that a disciplined testing of our emotions will uncover their inner rationality; will, indeed, uncover the laws imprinted in our hearts by the Creator. I take it that Lewis has the same intention in his remarks.

I believe that what Ignatius of Loyola calls the discernment of spirits aims at just such a disciplined testing of our feelings, our emotions, our values, our hearts. Hence, I will argue that if we want to address the spiritual and moral crisis of our times, all of us, and especially spiritual leaders, will have to challenge ourselves to engage in the discernment of spirits. If I am right, then spiritual leaders, spiritual directors and ministering people will have to encourage all of us, but especially men, to acknowledge our real feelings even when these feelings run counter to what we "should feel" and even to what religious doctrine says we "should feel." In other words, they will have to trust that discernment rather than mere obedience can give us the moral compass we need for our times.

What does the discernment of spirits mean? We can take some of the mystery out of the term if we reflect on how Ignatius learned discernment. In his *Autobiography* he tells us that while recovering from a very severe and painful leg wound, he engaged in two sets of daydreams. In one set he dreamed of doing great deeds as a knight and warrior and of winning the favor of a great lady. These daydreams would last for hours. In the meantime he had begun to read the life of Christ and a book of the lives of the saints, the only books in the castle. This reading led to another set of daydreams in which he dwelt on the imitation of the saints and the following of Christ. These daydreams also lasted for hours and alternated with the worldly ones. For some time Ignatius did not notice that these different dreams had different repercussions in his heart. While both sets of daydreams lasted, he felt exhilarated. However, when the worldly dreams ended, he felt sad, whereas when the dreams of following Christ and imitating the saints ended, he continued to feel content and happy. He did not notice the difference until one day, as he says,

> his eyes were opened a little, and he began to marvel at the difference and to reflect upon it, realizing from experience that some thoughts left him sad and others happy. Little by little he came to recognize the difference between the spirits that agitated him, one from the demon, the other from God (p. 23).

Obviously the discernment of spirits can take place in rather ordinary circumstances. Here Ignatius discerns God acting in daydreams, the kind of thing many of us do regularly. And discernment of spirits led to his conversion to a life of following Jesus.

With this first discernment we find most of the essentials of Ignatian spirituality and discernment. One of the hallmarks is the notion of finding God in all things. If God can be found in daydreams, then God can be found anywhere. Second, the human heart is a battleground where God and the evil one struggle. Third, God and the evil one engage in a relationship with each human being, each trying to draw the person to discipleship. Fourth, each one of us can notice the repercussions of these dialogical relationships in our experience. Fifth, we can discern in our experience what is of God from what is not of God. Finally, as a corollary, the only way to develop our discerning abilities is to let into our awareness all that goes on in our hearts. We must trust that God will lead us as he led Ignatius, by trial and error.

Ignatius could not find much help, except for an old woman, in his long and harrowing journey toward becoming a discerning person, but he did come to realize that some kind of spiritual direction could be very helpful to anyone who tried this way of developing a discerning heart. But the spiritual director, at least as director of the Spiritual Exercises, "should permit the Creator to deal directly with the creature, and the creature directly with his Creator and Lord." In other words, the spiritual director must encourage freedom in the person, a freedom to let feelings and thoughts and dreams come to the fore in order then to discern what is of God in them. Ignatius came to trust that an inner spiritual logic resides in our hearts, a dynamic that ultimately comes from the Holy Spirit dwelling in our hearts. The work of the director of the Spiritual Exercises consists in helping the retreatant discover that inner logic in him/herself. Thus, the process of Ignatian discernment helps a person to develop the kind of mature and realistic emotional life or heart that John Macmurray believes all of us, and especially men, need in order to meet the modern crisis.

For Macmurray feeling is more important than thought. He recognizes that masculine culture tends to disparage feeling, but he thinks the culture mistaken. "It is in the hands of feeling, not of thought, that the government of life should rest." He then notes that Jesus is on his side, "for he wished to make love—an emotion, not an idea—the basis of the good life" (p. 146). Feeling, he argues, is not blind and chaotic, but "has its own principle of order in itself, and will control and guide itself if it is given the chance" (p. 147). Macmurray merely affirms this principle of order. I believe that Ignatian spirituality with its emphasis on the discernment of spirits allows us to state that the principle of order is God's Holy Spirit dwelling in our hearts. Moreover, Macmurray does not offer a program for helping people to allow the principle of order to function. The principles of discernment elaborated by Ignatius give us such a program. This program is the "training of our emotional life" which Macmurray sees as so necessary if we are to meet the crisis of our times. Such discernment will so train the heart that we can come to know how to use the powerful tools our minds have put into our hands. For such discernment will attune our hearts with the one intention of God for our world. Then, indeed, our feelings, our hearts will be "rational" because they will be in tune with the reality which is this world of ours. Moreover, in our hearts fear for ourselves will be subordinated to love for others and for God.

Then, too, our actions can be more in tune with God's one action which is this world. For feeling is that in us which makes it possible for us to value things. "Good and evil," says Macmurray, "beauty and ugliness, significance and value of all kinds are apprehended by feeling, not by thought" (p. 147). Without feeling we would be unable to choose one thing over another, because we would not know how to value one or the other. If our feelings, our hearts are relatively in tune with God's one action which is this world, then we can choose to act in tune with that one action. Of course, we must also correctly assess the conditions of the world and thus use our minds. It is feeling, however, which motivates us to act at all, and feeling which is in tune with the Holy Spirit who is the Spirit of love in this world will motivate action that intends what God intends, a real community of love between all people. Faith, in the biblical sense, is precisely such feeling in tune with the Spirit. Someone may well wonder about the principle of obedience which was also dear to the heart of Ignatius. What I have been advocating seems to undermine the kind of obedience Ignatius, and the Catholic tradition, demand. Yet obedience can never become a substitute for personal responsibility. Our century has seen too many horrors justified by the argument that the perpetrator was only obeying orders. I would argue that obedience in the church requires that people strive to become adult discerners of the spirits. It requires adult and mature Christians who are not looking for a way to shirk personal responsibility and who can be fiercely honest with those in authority as well as respectful of them, as Ignatius himself was.

If religious leaders need to address the moral and spiritual crisis of our times, they need to do so not so much by calling us to blind obedience to church authority as by encouraging us to obey the inner dynamic of the Holy Spirit who dwells in our hearts and to communicate with one another the results of this obedience which is our discernment. Only adults whose hearts are in tune with the reality of God's world will be willing to face the dangers and opportunities of this world and to try to attune their actions and their institutions with the one intention or will of God. Only such adults can obey as Jesus obeyed. The process of attuning our hearts in this way through the discernment of spirits requires an openness to a continual conversion to a God who is always greater than our minds or hearts can fathom.

4

"Repent and Believe the Good News"

In Mark's gospel we read of the man possessed by the legion of demons.

> This man lived in the tombs, and no one could bind him any more, not even with a chain. For he had often been chained hand and foot, but he tore the chains apart and broke the irons on his feet. No one was strong enough to subdue him. Night and day among the tombs and in the hills he would cry out and cut himself with stones (Mk 5:3–5).

With these few lines the gospel writer has brought us face to face with madness personified. Here is someone who obviously did not and indeed could not believe in the good news. The demons which possessed him kept him bottled up in his own suffering and inner madness. I want to use this story as the starting point for an exploration of the difficulties many people have in believing the good news, of even beginning the process of conversion through discernment.

Before we take this topic up, however, let us first look at how we develop our image of ourselves in relationships with other people and with God. Psychologists indicate that we develop self-other schemata or images on the basis of experience. They postulate that the earliest experience of infants is one of almost cosmic unity where there are no distinctions between themselves and the rest of the world. Infants learn the difference between themselves and others gradually. What they learn are relationships. John, for example, learns that he is different from his mother but in relationship to her. And he discovers that he relates differently to his father than to his mother and that his father relates differently to him than his mother does. Over the course of years we develop a set of self-other images with which we approach new people in our lives. When we meet a stranger, we tend to assimilate that stranger into one of these self-other images. Thus psychologists explain instant likes and dislikes. If our self-other image structure is relatively flexible, we can learn a new way of relating from our experience with this stranger. If it is relatively rigid, we may learn nothing and thus act toward the stranger as though he or she were actually the other of our earlier experience. Thus psychologists explain the self-defeating behavior of people who repeatedly fall in love with the same kind of wrong persons for them. An example is the adult child of an alcoholic who marries an alcoholic, divorces him or her, and then falls in love with another person with alcoholic tendencies.

Our image of self-in-relationship-with-God also develops from our experiences with other people and from our experiences of God in church, through teaching, through chance remarks, and through prayer. Many people, however, retain an image of self-in-relationship-with-God that is relatively underdeveloped. Even though they develop relatively mature self-other images with which they face life, their image of God and self in

relation remains   pretty much what it was in childhood.
Depending on whether the image of God learned in
childhood was benign or malignant, they will approach
God in different ways, but in either case they will be
relating to an illusory God. If God is seen as benign, then
God may be approached as the giver of gifts such as good
weather for a picnic, good marks on an exam, etc. If,
however, God is seen as a snoop or a threatening poten-
tate, then he may not be approached at all. At most a
person with such an image of God might try to placate
God or to stay on God's good side by scrupulous adher-
ence to rules. The last remark brings us back to the man
possessed by the legion of demons.

The description of this man in Mark's gospel reminds me of many people who are torn apart by their
poor self-image and their feelings of being totally unworthy of God's love. A woman once told me that she could
not open the Bible without finding there condemnations
of herself. To me this meant that she had to pass over
page after page of the Bible where God speaks tenderly
even to sinners and promises them that though their sins
be scarlet they shall become whiter than snow. Scrupulous people are another case in point. They are torn apart
interiorly worrying about the least stray thought or
about whether they have particles of the host on their
hands after communion. Such people seem to have an
image of God as an ogre or a snoop ready to pounce upon
the slightest deviation from the straight and narrow.
They try by every means at their disposal to feel secure
before this terrifying God. If there are rules about behavior or thoughts, they try to follow them to the letter.
Paul the apostle seems to have been such a person before
his conversion. All of these efforts to achieve security
before God prove futile, of course. They just dig them-

selves into a deeper and deeper hole. Ignatius of Loyola contemplated suicide, for example. If they could be honest about how they felt toward this God, they would probably say that they hated him. In fact, it might be the beginning of the move toward a warmer, healthier relationship with God if they could express their anger. But they need a great deal of patient pastoral care to come to that point. Precisely such feelings of anger make them feel sinful before their implacable God.

People who have been hurt by life, especially in their early years, find it very difficult to believe in a God of love. I am thinking of the abused or abandoned child or the children of families ravaged by addiction to alcohol or drugs. Chaotic conditions in the family make it very hard for children to develop what Erikson calls "basic trust" both in life and in the Author of life. Their experience of the universe is not of a warm and homely place, but of a cruel, inconsistent and dangerous place. Moreover, it is not a place where their desires are consistently met. To ask for what you want could bring you a slap in the face just as easily as not. Such children could easily develop an image of God as a capricious, untrustworthy tyrant not to be trusted with one's deepest desires and hopes. Frequently enough such children are left with the impression that the family's problems are their fault. In such a case the tyrant God is righteously condemnatory. Our image of God is correlated with our image of ourselves.

People who have suffered painful losses in childhood also can develop an image of God as far from benevolent. Imagine a girl whose beloved father dies when she is five. Hardly comprehending what death means, but knowing that she will never see her father again, she hears someone say that God has taken him to himself.

One can easily imagine the image of God that could develop in her. The difficulty of her image of God in relationship to her could be compounded if she somehow or other imagines that she was responsible for God's action in taking her father. Suppose, for example, she had had a fit of anger at her father the day before he died.

People who have an image of God as an implacable tyrant or a snoop live in a world of illusion if what we said in the first chapter is true. If they are to repent and believe the good news, they must somehow turn away from the illusory God and toward the real God. Easier said than done, however. Sermons and exhortations stressing the goodness and kindness of God may help, but often enough only minimally. Self-other images that are rigid and lead to self-defeating behavior are very difficult to change because they are continually being reinforced by the self-defeating behavior. So, too, rigid self-God images are continually being reinforced. There are powerful images in the Bible, for example, of God's implacable anger at a sinful people and sinful individuals. God wipes out Sodom and Gomorrah because he cannot find even ten good people there. Though David's own life is spared when he repents of sleeping with Uriah's wife and of having Uriah killed, the baby born of the illicit union with Bathsheba must die. I still remember my feeling that some injustice was at work when I first heard or read the story of Uzzah who was struck dead by God because he reached out to save the Ark from toppling off the cart when David was bringing it up to Jerusalem (2 Sam 6:6–7). And some Christian theologians have argued that God's justice demanded that Jesus die to appease God's wrath. The woman who could not open the Bible without finding condemnation there was at least a bit right. Moreover, life can be capricious and cruel. A woman who had with great difficulty just begun to experience God as kind and merciful found out that her daughter had leukemia and was once again plunged into feelings of self-hatred, believing that her sinfulness had drawn the ire of God upon her family. What can be done to overcome the illusory image of God?

First, such people need experiences that point to a different image of God. No matter how cruel life has been, everyone meets at least some people who are kind and good. Too often we concentrate on the bad news and miss the good news that is also present every day. I have often found that people who have been hurt early in life still remember someone who was kind to them. Remembering such a person helps them to recognize that there have been some silver linings in their otherwise cloudy days. The memory may also be of an experience of the kind of Joy C. S. Lewis describes. In Anne Tyler's novel *Dinner at the Homesick Restaurant,* Pearl Tull is a dying old woman whose husband abandoned her and their three children. Her life has been very hard, and it has taken a toll on her, making her crotchety and nagging. Her eldest son wants nothing to do with her. She begins to go blind. Near the end of her life she asks her son Ezra, with whom she is living, to read to her from her childhood diary. It's as though she wants to remember something. She keeps gesturing him to go on. The diary entries are pretty banal. "Move on," she tells him. Then comes this paragraph.

> He riffled through the pages, glimpsing "buttonhole stitch" and "watermelon social" and "set of fine furs for $22.50." "Early this morning," he read to his mother, "I went out behind the house to weed. Was kneeling in the dirt by

the stable with my pinafore a mess and perspiration rolling down my back, wiped my face on my sleeve, reached for the trowel, and all at once thought, Why I believe that at just this moment I am absolutely happy."
His mother stopped rocking and grew still.
"The Bedloe girl's piano scales were floating out her window," he read, "and a bottle fly was buzzing in the grass, and I saw that I was kneeling on such a beautiful green little planet. I don't care what else might come about, I have had this moment. It belongs to me."
That was the end of the entry. He fell silent.
"Thank you, Ezra," his mother said. "There's no need to read any more."

The next page in the novel announces her death. It seems that she wanted to remember that moment before she died. I suspect that many people have such experiences. They are, I believe, the affective foundation for a desire to develop a closer relationship with God.

Very scrupulous people find it extremely difficult to focus on God as a benign figure as we have already said. God is a snoop. They tend to recoil from a psalm such as Psalm 139. Imagine someone with an image of God as a snoop hearing these lines.

O Lord, you have searched me and you know me.
You know when I sit and when I rise;
    you perceive my thoughts from afar.
You discern my going out and my lying down;
    you are familiar with all my ways.
Before a word is on my tongue

you know it completely, O Lord
(Ps 139:1–4).

I have known people who reacted with horror and depression to these words. Spiritual directors have to be careful what they suggest to people with scruples. Even this psalm which many people read as an affirmation of God's loving care can be misinterpreted because of a particular self-God image a person has. With such persons I have tried to find out what experiences they enjoy and have tried to help them to associate such experiences with God.

People with a negatively charged image of self-in-relationship-with-God are also helped if they can come to the point of expressing their anger at the hurts that life and, supposedly, the Author of life has dealt them. It may be frightening at first to admit to oneself and to God that I do not trust him, but it can be the beginning of a changed experience of God. One scrupulous man I directed seemed to be angry as he talked about the compulsive rituals he felt he had to go through. I asked him whether he liked this God. He blurted out how much he hated God and all this ritual. This outburst, it seemed to me, was the beginning of his conversion from the illusory image of God he harbored. When people tell me that they told God off in no uncertain terms, I usually ask them how God seemed to them. The question sometimes takes them aback, but when they reflect on the experience, they say things like, "I didn't feel threatened," "He seemed to listen," "I felt that he sympathized with me." Such experiences help them to trust that God actually does want to hear their real reactions to what has happened in their lives.

Some people who express their resentment at God

have experienced God as deeply sympathetic toward
what happened to them in life and have felt that the
following poem expresses what God communicated
to them.

One night I had a dream—
I dreamed I was walking along the beach with
    the Lord and
Across the sky flashed scenes from my life.
For each scene I noticed two sets of footprints
    in the sand.
One belonged to me and the other to the Lord.
When the last scene of my life flashed before
    me,
I looked back at the footprints in the sand.
I noticed that many times along the path of my
    life
There was only one set of footprints.
I also noticed that it happened at the very
    lowest and saddest times of my life.
This really bothered me and I questioned the
    Lord about it.
"Lord, you said that once I decided to follow
    you,
You would walk with me all the way.
But I have noticed that during the most
    troublesome times in my life
There is only one set of footprints.
I don't understand why in times when I needed
    you most, you should leave me."
The Lord replied, "My precious, precious
    child, I love you and I would never leave
    you during your times of trial and
    suffering.

When you saw only one set of footprints,
It was then that I carried you" (Author
unknown).

Sometimes humor helps. Recently I heard of a story
from a medieval Jewish commentary on the opening
chapters of the Book of Genesis. The commentary indi-
cated that the creation story in Genesis was actually
God's twenty-seventh try, the first twenty-six having
been total failures. As the Lord God started this twenty-
seventh attempt, he spoke these words: "Let's hope it
works." The humor indicates that human beings have
been trying to make sense of all the "good" and "bad" of
this universe. If people can laugh at such a joke or recognize that rather pious people can do so, then they may
begin to have a different experience of God.

And when all is said and done, only a different experience of God will change our illusory images of God
and God's relationship to us and our world. Spiritual
directors, pastoral counselors and other ministers need
to bend every effort to help people with deeply illusory
images of God to have experiences of the real God. In
various writings I have referred to a wonderful paragraph by a British psychiatrist, J. S. Mackenzie.

The *enjoyment of God* should be the supreme
end of spiritual technique; and it is in that enjoyment of God that we feel not only saved
in the Evangelical sense, but safe: we are
conscious of belonging to God, and hence are
never alone; and, to the degree we have these
two, hostile feelings disappear. . . . In that relationship Nature seems friendly and homely;
even its vast spaces instead of eliciting a sense

of terror speak of the infinite love; and the nearer beauty becomes the garment with which the Almighty clothes Himself.

Many people need all the ingenuity ministers can muster to help them to experience God as enjoyable.

In this unbelievably complex universe not only does the earth produce abundantly so that human life is possible, but also earthquakes and hurricanes, cancers, embolisms and genetic defects occur. A universe such as ours, it seems, is impossible without the "bad" as well as the "good" events. Moreover, the same free will that allows humans to love one another also allows horrors such as the Holocaust, the gulags, the "killing fields," the senseless cruelty of human beings toward one another, the physical and sexual abuse of children, and the rape and abuse of the environment on such a massive scale in this century. Human life, for all its wonders and joys and exuberance, includes sickness, suffering, sin and death. But, some will say, these specters entered our world with sin; sickness, suffering and death are thus not natural, but the results of human perversity. Some modern theologians would argue, however, that sin did not bring suffering and death into the world; rather it changed the way we experience suffering and death. Thus sin did not bring death into the world; sin brought the terror of death into our midst. On this understanding sickness and death are part and parcel of being human in an imperfect world.

In this complex universe, therefore, where suffering and death come from "natural" causes as well as from the stupidity and cruelty of human beings, Christians believe that God continually works to bring about his intention which is the community of all human beings with the Trinity and one another. In "good" times or in "bad" God is interested in bringing about community, in helping human beings to love one another.

Is God, then, indifferent, even callous to human suffering as many of the people we have been discussing in this chapter seem to implicitly believe? One way to help such people is to point them to the example of Jesus. We believe that Jesus is the enfleshment of God, the Second Person of God in human flesh. We can get some grasp of God's reactions to human suffering by contemplating Jesus' reactions in the gospels. A leper said to Jesus: "If you are willing, you can make me clean." "Filled with compassion, Jesus reached out his hand and touched the man. 'I am willing,' he said. 'Be clean' " (Mk 1:40–41). In John's gospel we read that Jesus was deeply moved and troubled when Mary spoke to him about her brother Lazarus' death and wept when he came to the grave (Jn 11:33–35). If Jesus really is an indicator of God's reactions, then God is not indifferent to our suffering. People may come to have a different experience of God's reality through reflecting on and contemplating those passages in the gospels where Jesus is so obviously moved to compassion.

The conversion from illusion about God and oneself in the world does not come easily. It requires that we give up our resentments at what we have suffered in life. I can recall an incident in my own life when I came to realize that my healing required that I accept reality. A friend and I had come to a point in our relationship where it was clear that we needed to relate differently. I had become too demanding of my friend's time. I was upset and angry and unhappy. I prayed for healing and came upon the passage in Matthew's gospel where two blind men follow Jesus into a house asking to be healed.

Jesus asked them, "Do you believe that I am able to do this?" (Mt 9:28). I suddenly realized that if I said "Yes," I would be healed, but it would also mean that I would have to give up my resentments and my hidden desire that nothing change in the relationship. This felt to me like losing the relationship entirely. The best I could do at the time was to ask Jesus to give me the desire to be healed. Since that time I have come to realize that many of our self-defeating behaviors which are based on un- derdeveloped self-other images die very hard precisely because they are self-images. To change the image seems to mean a death to the relationship and, therefore, a death to the self. I often liken the difficulty to that of a soldier in a foxhole. He may be in terrible danger and may be told that across that bridge covered with fog he will find safety. But the foxhole is his and bears his stamp and smell. It may be dangerous, but at least he knows the devil he has. It takes a lot of courage to ask for healing of life's hurts.

All the "spiritual techniques" we have been discuss- ing in this chapter aim to help people to a conversion, a turning away from an image of God as cruel or implaca- ble or just distant, and a turning toward the real God who is love, indeed self-sacrificing love. They are ways of helping people to "repent and believe the good news." The process for men and women who have been scarred by life as was the man possessed by the legion of demons can be long and arduous. They themselves need patience and those who minister to them also need pa- tience and great kindness. Neither group is left bereft, however. The deepest reality of this world is always God's creative action who desires to communicate his life and love at every moment of the world's existence.

Gerard Manley Hopkins expressed this idea in his won-
derfully pregnant poem "God's Grandeur."

> The world is charged with the grandeur of God.
>   It will flame out, like shining from shook
>   foil;
>   It gathers to a greatness, like the ooze of oil
> Crushed. Why do men then now not reck his
>   rod?
> Generations have trod, have trod, have trod;
>   And all is seared with trade; bleared,
>   smeared with toil;
>   And wears man's smudge and shares man's
>   smell: the soil
> Is bare now, nor can foot feel, being shod.
>
> And for all this, nature is never spent;
>   There lives the dearest freshness deep
>   down things;
> And though the last lights off the black West
>   went
>   Oh, morning, at the brown brink
>   eastward, springs—
> Because the Holy Ghost over the bent
>   World broods with warm breast and with
>   ah! bright wings.

The last image beautifully evokes the world both as an
egg pregnant with life being warmed by the Holy Spirit
and as bent in the sense of out of shape, sinful, somehow
not what God intended. This is the real God at the heart
of the universe, the good news all spiritual technique
aims to make present so that we can turn from illusion
to reality.

5

"You Are the Man!"

King David fell in love with Bathsheba, the wife of Uriah the Hittite, and slept with her. When she became pregnant and he could not induce Uriah to sleep with his wife, he ordered Joab, the commander of the troops besieging Rabbah, to put Uriah in the center of the battle and then leave him alone so that he would be killed. After this terrible deed Nathan the prophet told David a parable about a rich man who took the only lamb a poor man had instead of using one of his own large flock to feed a traveler. "David burned with anger against the man and said to Nathan, 'As surely as the Lord lives, the man who did this deserves to die!' " Nathan then said to David, "You are the man!" And David replied, "I have sinned against the Lord" (2 Sam 11–12).

David's confession of sin has become almost a paradigm of repentance or conversion. He admits the guilt which has alienated him from God and thus turns back to God. In the last chapter we spoke of a conversion from an illusory image of God to an image that more nearly squares with the reality of God's self-revelation. In this chapter we will be looking at the conversion from another illusion. However, the terms are different. A man who was physically abused in childhood is not guilty of what happened to him. If he is converted to the good news, he will not have to repent of his childhood although he may come to realize that he had been guilty of holding onto his resentment at life's hurts almost as a way of getting even with his abusers or with God ("See what you've done to me"). In the present instance, however, David is guilty. When he says, "I have sinned against the Lord," he is only admitting the truth. But we will see that this conversion requires a twofold conversion from illusion. David first had to be convicted of the truth of his guilt and to turn away from his sinful behavior. But sinners also have to give up the illusion that God does not continue to love them even as sinners.

In the rules for discernment of spirits in the *Spiritual Exercises* Ignatius of Loyola starts as follows:

> Rules for understanding to some extent the different movements produced in the soul and for recognizing those that are good to admit them, and those that are bad, to reject them. . . .
> 1. In the case of those who go from one mortal sin to another, the enemy is ordinarily accustomed to propose apparent pleasures. He fills their imagination with sensual delights and gratifications, the more readily to keep them in their vices and increase the number of their sins.
> With such persons the good spirit uses a method which is the reverse of the above. Making use of the light of reason, he will rouse the sting of conscience and fill them with remorse.

Let us use the story of David to illustrate Ignatius' points. David had committed a heinous crime. Not only had he committed adultery with another man's wife while that man was serving him in war at risk of his life, but he had also, in effect, had the man killed. The apparent pleasures of satisfying his lust led to Bathsheba's pregnancy. David tried to get himself off the hook by inducing Uriah to sleep with his wife. In other words, David wanted the baby to seem to be Uriah's. He did not want to admit to the truth and take responsibility for his actions. None of his stratagems worked. Uriah refused, because of his oath as a soldier, to go home at night to his wife. In his blindness David cast around for a way out of his predicament and hit upon a terrible solution, one that many men with power have used throughout history. Perhaps he said to himself, "A king is above the law; his prestige is necessary to protect the nation itself." So David decided to write a letter to Joab telling him to let Uriah be killed in battle. One sin led to another, much as Ignatius predicts. The strategy of temptation outlined by Ignatius brought David to jeopardize not only the life of Uriah, but also the lives of many of his soldiers. Indeed, in the ensuing battle many other soldiers were killed along with Uriah. Even when Joab's messenger told David that a number of David's soldiers had been killed, all he had to add are the words, "Moreover, your servant Uriah the Hittite is dead," for David to reply, "Say this to Joab: 'Don't let this upset you; the sword devours one as well as another' " (2 Sam 11:24–25). Up to this point in the story David showed not a hint of remorse. He seemed totally blind to the evil he had done. Illusion reigned in his heart.

When Ignatius writes of the strategy of the "good spirit," he reminds us of a truth we often do not recognize. Only God can reveal a sinful state to us. Sin, precisely as such, is a turning away from reality. In the process of turning away from reality we do have qualms of conscience, but once we have done the deed, blindness sets in. We have all kinds of rationalizations for our actions, and these rationalizations blind us to the state we are in. We can live in the illusion of innocence. Thus David could hear the parable Nathan told and not have a clue that the parable applied to him. In this state of blindness and illusion only God can open our inner eyes to the truth.

Of course, in our need to continue to be blind to the reality of our sinfulness we have many helpers. Ignatius speaks of the "enemy" or the "evil spirit." Our age has a tendency to downplay the reality of Satan. Screwtape, C. S. Lewis' senior devil, notes in one of *The Screwtape Letters* that the "High Command" has decided that "(o)ur policy, for the moment, is to conceal ourselves." Given the horrors our century has witnessed, it is rather amazing that this strategy seems to be succeeding. We can, it is true, become too preoccupied with the devil, and indeed, Lewis indicates that such a preoccupation also plays into the devil's hands. However, a healthy belief in the existence of Satan may save us from lengthier periods of blindness. But we also have helpers in our culture. Much of our media and advertising are, consciously or unconsciously, geared to keep us in a state of blindness to our sinful state. David would have had much to reassure him about the naturalness of his adulterous conduct if he had been able to watch American television. And the "end justifies the means" philosophy that seems to be the justification for the killing of innocent civilians in modern war ("We had to destroy the village in order to save it") and to have lurked behind the sordid events surrounding the Watergate scandal might well have comforted his conscience as he decided to despatch Uriah. Rationalizations for every kind of turning away from God's dream for our universe and ourselves abound in our culture, and perhaps have abounded ever since the first sin. In the Genesis account Adam blames Eve and Eve blames the serpent.

It takes a powerful statement from Nathan to open David's eyes. "You are the man!" And Nathan proceeds to deliver God's judgment on David's actions. God reveals to David that he is a sinner, that he has deliberately fallen short of the dream God has for him, but God's revelation comes through the mediation of Nathan. David, like the rest of us, needs not only the revelation of God but also the intervention of a real friend who tells him the truth. Many addicts have finally had the blinders removed by the intervention of friends who without condemnation told them the truth. Such interventions, I believe, are the fruits of God's Holy Spirit impelling friends to be real friends and thus are the instruments of God's revelation of the truth.

It is just as important to note that we do have helpers that move us to conversion as that we have helpers to keep us blind. Once again we can miss the good news because of a concentration on the bad. There are elements in our culture and our surroundings that continually remind us of reality. The same media that seem to try to beguile us into remaining in our illusions also present us with the evidence that all is not right with our world and with ourselves. The churches which can be helpers to our blindness since they are, after all, ourselves, also do often speak the unpopular truth that the "emperor has no clothes." And at the heart of the universe, we believe, is the pulsing love of God, the Holy Spirit who tries to draw all of us away from illusion to the bright reality of God's dream.

Ignatius' second rule for the discernment of spirits takes up the actions of the two opposing spirits with those who earnestly strive to live according to God's dream.

> Then it is characteristic of the evil spirit to harass with anxiety, to afflict with sadness, to raise obstacles backed by fallacious reasonings that disturb the soul. Thus he seeks to prevent the soul from advancing.
>
> It is characteristic of the good spirit, however, to give courage and strength, consolations, tears, inspirations, and peace. This He does by making all easy, by removing all obstacles so the soul goes forward in doing good.

For example, the recovering addict who wants to continue sobriety hears the siren call, "How can you live without a fix for the rest of your life?" Ignatius himself was afflicted with such a siren call when an interior voice asked him how he could live this life of asceticism for the seventy years he had to live. He had the grace to respond, "Can you promise me one hour of life?" just as members of Alcoholics Anonymous are urged to respond, "One day at a time." The grace of God gave him the courage and desire to continue this life which he believed led to his own greatest happiness.

A recent novel rather cogently portrays the pull toward conversion from a life of illusion to a life of hope and reality. In *Vestments* by Alfred Alcorn, Sebastian Taggart seems to have life at his finger tips. He is living with a classy and wealthy woman in a fashionable apartment in the Boston area. His job as editorial writer for the most popular Boston T.V. station brings him some renown and even a sense that he is doing some good. That all is not right with Sebastian shows itself in his excessive drinking. The aunt who took him from an English orphanage and brought him up a Catholic in Boston is dying in a nursing home. As she moves in and out of reality, she imagines that Sebastian has become the priest she always dreamed he would be. Perhaps to console her, perhaps to insure that he would not lose his inheritance, Sebastian takes to wearing clerical garb. The novel can be seen as the struggle that goes on in Sebastian between the pulls toward illusion and toward reality.

The thoughts of the wealth he hopes to inherit from his aunt prompt him to daydream about a life of luxury and high culture, of fast cars and sleek women. Then the novelist writes:

> And yet. And yet, for all his daydreams, or perhaps because of them, some essence of freedom eluded him. No incarnation of the abstraction quite sufficed. After the fantasies had reeled through his mind like so many feature films he could summon at will, he would end with a profound sense of ennui, of having ransacked his possible futures. It was as if he could imagine all too well the things he wanted in life and, in imagining them, live them, emptying them of their promise. He had the awful suspicion at times that wealth wouldn't suffice, that it would only be more of what he already had—more things, more privileges, more time.

This is one set of daydreams, of living a life even more elegant than his present one, and it leaves him dry and bored.

Something strange happens when he puts on the

clerical clothes. As he drove his car, he loosened the scarf which was covering the clerical collar.

> As he did so, an extraordinarily benign mood settled on him. He edged out into the flow of cars along Memorial Drive and found himself suddenly and inexplicably at peace with the world, found himself driving like a gentleman, observing vehicular courtesies with decorous, clerical nods of the head. Other drivers, he noticed, especially if they saw the collar, returned the civilities. He resisted an impulse to reach for a cigarette. He didn't need it or the cold beer he had packed along.

In the course of the novel Sebastian begins to think of becoming a priest. The only problem is that he does not believe in God. However, the reactions he has while wearing the collar keep tugging at him, giving him hope and a sense of reality in a way that puzzles him.

Sebastian tries to save himself. He gives up drinking and begins to go to church. He leads a semi-monastic life. He even begins to work in a shelter for homeless street people. But faith eludes him.

Near the end of the novel he goes on a long bender and almost burns down the shelter because he is drunk when he comes to work. In despair he drinks even more and plans his suicide. In a drunken dream he believes that he has actually carried it out only to wake up the next morning on the floor of his room. "He saw himself rescued from certain self-destruction and tears of relief stung his eyes." Then he remembers with self-loathing the day before when he almost burned down the shelter.

He reaches for a nearly empty bottle of whiskey. As he
unscrews the cap, he asks himself,

> . . . yet why the joy . . . if life is merely a misery
> to be blotted out? In that swoon of relief, just
> moments ago, he had nearly wept for being
> alive. Do I simply fear death? There had to be
> more to it than that. As he recalled the feeling,
> it returned. It was like love, not of self, but of
> being. It made his life, any life, seem a gift of
> incalculable wonder. He put the bottle down
> and screwed the top back on. Life suddenly
> seemed to brim with possibilities. He was
> happy with a happiness that, as he invoked it,
> took on a momentum of its own.

Moreover, he realizes that he does have faith in God's
love and, unlike his other delusions, this faith remains
and begins to take deeper and deeper root in him. Finally
he recognizes that this faith had been there all the time,
"deep in his heart, a legacy, but one smothered by pride,
greed, and the myriad distractions of the world." Sebastian has finally come home to the reality that had been
pursuing him throughout the novel.

Sebastian, like all of us sinners, had to face the
truth. He had to acknowledge that he was an alcoholic
and also a sinner, and that like Francis Thompson he had
been fleeing God "down the nights and down the days"
and "down the arches of the years." But the other truth
he had to face and accept was that God had been pursuing him "with unhurrying chase,/And unperturbèd
pace." Finally, again like Thompson, he heard and accepted God's words.

'Ah, fondest, blindest, weakest,
I am He whom thou seekest!
Thou dravest love from thee, who dravest Me.'
    (*The Hound of Heaven*)

In other words, until he could accept that God in Christ
was his loving savior in spite of, or even because of his
sins, Sebastian could not accept his own reality. At the
beginning of this chapter we spoke of a twofold turning
from illusion. Accepting the truth of my sinfulness and
accepting the reality of God's continued love of me the
sinner go hand in hand.

The example of Peter in the gospels may give us an
idea of what this twofold conversion means. In Luke's
gospel Peter first meets Jesus when Jesus uses his boat to
teach the people. After Jesus finished speaking, he told
Peter to go out fishing again. Although they had caught
nothing the night before, Peter put out the boat at Jesus'
request and "they caught such a large number of fish
that their nets began to break." "When Peter saw this,
he fell at Jesus' knees and said, 'Go away from me, Lord;
I am a sinful man' " (Lk 5:1-8). Quite clearly Peter's
sense of sinfulness has not come from a revelation of the
Lord. Jesus eats with tax collectors and sinners. Indeed,
he scandalizes the "better types" by fraternizing with
harlots and suchlike. When Jesus reveals sinfulness and
the other person accepts that reality, they sit down and
have a festive meal. Jesus does not drive them away. So
Peter's reaction is based on an illusion.

Many people react the way Peter reacted. They feel
that God and Jesus would not want anything to do with
them because of their sins. On retreats when they contemplate the washing of the feet in John's gospel (13:1-
9), they recoil as Peter did. They feel unworthy to let

Jesus wash their feet. The illusion here is that Jesus cares about worthiness. He wants to serve his disciples, to do a loving act for them, and he knows quite well who they are and what kind of men and women they are.

In John 21 we see the exquisite tact of Jesus in revealing not only the reality of Peter's sin but also of Jesus' own continued love and trust of Peter. I may be reading too much into the repeated question of Jesus, "Do you love me?" but when Peter responds each time, not with apologies and fear, nor even with comparisons of himself to others, but with the protestation, "You know that I love you," perhaps Jesus breathes a sigh of relief. "You finally have understood me." My own experience with the contemplation of this text gave me this insight.

For years I confessed sins almost by rote, practically the same catalogue each time. It never occurred to me to ask God to help me to know my own sinfulness. As a result of these confessions nothing much ever changed. I thought that I considered myself a sinner, but now I'm not so sure. I believe that I was revealing my own "sins" to myself, not letting God reveal to me his vision of me. The focus was on me, not on God and God's forgiving love. But one time on retreat as I contemplated this scene in John 21, I felt that Jesus wanted me to tell him that I loved him. I knew that he was aware of my faults, my cowardice, and my sinfulness, but he seemed to want me to tell him that I loved him. In other words, it seemed important to him. I felt a great sense of freedom and release and a burst of love for him which I put into words. I realized that my sins and sinful tendencies are not obstacles to intimacy with him. In a real sense I heard Jesus say to me, "You are the man." "You are the man who cowardly failed to stand up for someone who was being maligned; you are the man who. . . . etc.'' But I felt these statements as balm for my heart because Jesus loved me and wanted me to love him. Moreover, I felt empowered to ask for the grace to change these sinful behaviors and tendencies.

Now more often than not, I can laugh at my faults and failures and ask for real forgiveness and a change of heart. Even as I write this book, I can fall into moments when I begin to admire some of my writing skill, when I begin to think that the worth of the book depends wholly on me. When that happens, I frequently find myself getting anxious and worried that I will not get it done by the deadline or that it will fall flat. It is rather perverse, is it not? I am writing a book about conversion to the living God, yet I fall back into self-absorption. Now, however, I seem more able to turn to Jesus with a smile and a shrug and a sense that he, too, shrugs with a sort of wry smile. I can ask him to be with me and guide me. Then my anxieties seem to disappear and my thoughts and associations run more freely. Moreover, I feel something like a comic relief to know that Jesus is bemused, too, by my foolishness. There is nothing I can do about my sinfulness except to ask God to continue to reveal the truth to me even when I resist, to help me to repent and to continue to assure me that he loves me warts and all.

6

"I Didn't Mean to Hurt Anybody."

In the movie *Alfie* Michael Caine plays a footloose Don Juan type, a con man and seducer. I saw it years ago, but one line sticks in my memory. Near the end of the movie Alfie says something like, "I never want to hurt anyone." Whoever he is talking to responds, "But you do, Alfie, you do." One of the persistent illusions we harbor is that our failures to live according to God's dream for us have no consequences beyond ourselves. The desire for God that is our deepest desire has to burst the bubble of that illusion. But it is not an easy task.

The first eleven chapters of the Book of Genesis can be read as the story of the consequences of the alienation from God's dream brought on by the sin of Adam and Eve. In chapter four Cain, in a fit of jealousy, kills his brother Abel and then lies to God's face. God asks him where his brother is, and Cain replies, "I don't know. Am I my brother's keeper?" (Gen 4:9) In chapter five we note that people die at younger and younger ages. In chapter six evil has become so rampant that God decides to send a flood to destroy humankind. Chapters six through ten tell the story of the flood and how God saved Noah and his family and two of each living creature on the face of the earth in the ark. Even after the covenant God makes with Noah the effects of evil do not cease. In chapter eleven the pride of human beings leads God to confuse their tongues so that now they are separated, not only by their fears and jealousies and hatreds, but also by their inability to understand one another. God's dream of a world where all persons will live in community with one another because they are in community with God seems shattered. The consequences of human actions are fateful indeed.

As children we learned the ditty, "Sticks and stones will break my bones, but names will never hurt me." Don't believe it. Names do hurt, and the hurt can have long-range consequences. I still cringe when I remember that as a boy I blurted out in her presence a particularly nasty nickname some boys had pinned on a girl in grammar school. I hope that the scar I caused to her psyche has healed. In my work as a counselor and spiritual director I have met many people who have been scarred by cutting and demeaning remarks made to them as children, leaving them with a poor self-image which has had deleterious effects on their lives. Names do hurt, and it is an illusion and a rationalization to deny the fact.

The proliferation of Twelve-Step programs for people who were sexually abused as children and for the adult children of alcoholics are reminders that there are generational consequences to our actions. Moreover, it is well-known that addiction and child abuse run in families. Often enough an addict deludes him/herself that the addiction only does the addict harm. Steps eight and nine of the steps toward recovery in Alcoholics Anonymous are to make an inventory of those one has hurt and to try to make amends to them. Whether the apology is accepted or not is not the point; the point is to admit the truth. It is another step in the conversion process.

This reference to Twelve-Step programs reminds

me of the process Ignatius of Loyola suggests to retreatants who have become aware of their sinfulness. Ignatius presupposes that they have the desire to know the
full nature of their sinful actions and has them beg God
to reveal to them their sins and the consequences of
them so that they can repent of them and believe the
good news that God still loves the sinner. Ignatius had
learned from his own experience how healing it was to
let God reveal his sins to him. He had spent some time
battling with scruples about his sins, wondering if he
had confessed them all and fully. He was in such agony
that he contemplated suicide. He finally came to realize
that these scrupulous thoughts and feelings were a
temptation. When God reveals our sins and sinful tendencies to us, his purpose is to bring us to conversion
from them and from the alienation they produce, a conversion to the peace that surpasses all understanding.
Ignatius also realized that it is profoundly healing if we
take the time to let God reveal to us in detail how we
have "fallen short of the glory of God." The more we
understand and feel the reality of what we have done
and been, the more firmly we will want to reform our
lives and the more convinced we will be of God's continued love for us sinners. Moreover, we will come to
know deeply that God's forgiveness is not "cheap
grace," but "tough love." God's love does not blind him
to reality, and God knows, it seems, that our own deepest happiness lies in seeing ourselves and our world as
God does.

After they beg God to reveal to them their sins so
that they can deeply know themselves and repent, Ignatius suggests that retreatants spend time making an inventory of their sins and sinful tendencies. They go

through their lives in their minds and imaginations expecting that God will show them what they need to know about themselves. They can do this in stages, taking time with each period of their lives. It is important to recognize the purpose of this exercise. It is not primarily to draw up a laundry list of sins for a general confession. Nor is it to be an exercise in self-absorption. The self-absorbed examination of sins can become a way of resisting the light of God's love and of God's view of one's sinfulness. Witness the self-scrutiny of the scrupulous person. The primary purpose of this exercise is to know the truth, to overcome the illusions and rationalizations that keep us from the deepest desire of our hearts, union with God and one another. Each of us harbors some secrets, some sins, some deviant actions that we are ashamed of, even if we are not fully conscious of them. That shame keeps us from full transparency before God, keeps us in fear of being found out, as it were. We are, like Adam and Eve, "in hiding," as William Reiser puts it. Only after they had eaten of the fruit of the tree of good and evil did they put on clothes. "I heard you in the garden, and I was afraid because I was naked; so I hid" (Gen 3:10). The failures and sins of our past lives keep us in hiding from God, and we may not even know why we are so afraid of closeness to the very One who is our deepest love.

As we let God reveal to us who we really have been and are, Ignatius expects that we will feel shame and sorrow. He hopes that we will even weep for what we have done and be moved to take steps to change our behavior. People also feel moved to apologize to those they have hurt. Sometimes the apologies have to be made in prayer because those who have been hurt are dead. I have known people who have openly spoken to those who have died and experienced a new and freer relationship with them, whether they were parents or others whom they have hurt. They felt forgiven and loved by them as well as by God. In fact, speaking to these dead people whom they had hurt made more real the presence of God. After my mother's death, for example, I realized that she now knew more about me than I would ever have told her in life. I did not feel threatened by the thought. That realization brought me up short, and I had to admit that somehow, in spite of my theology, I actually felt that there were secrets I could keep from God.

Of course, not all the people we have hurt in our lives are dead. During this inventory taking we come to recognize that there are people whom we have hurt, and we often feel the desire to make amends in some way. It is not easy, but it may be worth our while for our own peace of mind, if for no other reason, to do the difficult thing. If we do take some steps, either in person or in writing, we need to remind ourselves, as the ninth Step of Alcoholics Anonymous does, that the point is to take the step whether or not the other accepts my effort of amendment. This is wise advice because our ability to delude ourselves is so strong. We could be taking the step to assure ourselves that the past was just a bad dream. God has been revealing reality to us, not a bad dream. Reality and our deepest happiness ask that we say, "I did it. I actually hurt you."

Ignatius has an interesting point in this exercise. He seems to expect that retreatants will be astonished that the universe has been so good and kind to them in spite of the warped nature of their behavior.

Why have the angels, though they are the word
of God's justice, tolerated me, guarded me, and
prayed for me! Why have the saints interceded
for me and asked favors for me! And the
heavens, sun, moon, stars, and the elements;
the fruits, birds, fishes, and other animals—
why have they all been at my service!

Depending on one's mood (or bias) one can read this
outburst as either dark, brooding and self-lacerating or
as joyful and buoyant. Since Ignatius is described by
those who lived with him as a joyful, lively man, I
choose to read the text as describing joyful astonish-
ment. Indeed I am reminded of Sebastian Taggart's joy
mentioned in the last chapter, a joy "like love, not of
self, but of being. It made his life, any life, seem a gift of
incalculable wonder." The joy is, I believe, the joy of
realizing that in spite of all one's folly and sin one is still
embraced by the love that desires the universe into existence. The deepest reality of the universe has not been
altered by our sins. What a wonder that is!

To come to this experience of joy we must be willing to go through what may be a "dark valley." We resist
very strongly facing our responsibility for hurting
others, or bringing pain and suffering into our world. So
the experience of joy may be a long time in coming, but
it is time well spent. Many experience tears of joy as they
feel themselves to be loved sinners. We need to stress
that they *experience* this joy; they do not tell themselves
that they are saved. For many the experience is like a
baptism, like a new birth, and now they know, perhaps
for the first time, what it means to be saved. The knowledge is a deep, abiding, felt kind of thing ("knowledge"

in the way John means the word in his gospel). It is the kind of knowing that leads to action and desire, the kind of knowing that wants to be shared and spread. It is "good news."

It is often thought that therapy works because the patient grubs around in his past and finds the "cause" of his symptoms; but in actuality what happens, I believe, is that here and now in the therapy I find that I no longer need to fear myself or the other person as I had, and so I can deal with people on a more mature level. True enough, I come to realize that I have been dealing with people as though I were a five-year-old boy, and I may even realize why I did that. But the real change comes when I realize now and experience *now* that I am an adult talking to and reacting to another adult. So, too, with the experience of repentance we have been discussing. It is not the remembering of all my past sins alone that heals, but the experience of being saved from my present alienation from God and other people because of the effects of these sins on me and others.

The conversion to reality which we have been stressing may also be illumined by a reflection on the therapy process. I believe that in successful therapy with neurotics (successful in the sense of leading to deep change of the neurotic patterns) there comes a point when clients come to recognize their own complicity in their neurosis and their own covert gratification through their symptoms. For example, I recall one man who wore a kind of secret smile as he described how a friend had blown up at him. He came to realize that he took a sort of perverse pleasure in goading friends into rejecting him. Of course, there were traumatic events in his past that were the precipitating factors in his neurosis, and of course, he was for the most part unaware that he took pleasure in his own self-defeating dynamics. Still, he came to recognize his own complicity in maintaining his self-defeating behavior. In this day when we are so aware of diminished guilt, it is well to be aware of this subtlety because otherwise we can too quickly make excuses for and too easily reassure ourselves and others without allowing ourselves and them to come to terms with our own sense of guilt and shame for our own real part in the sinfulness and pain there is in our world.

Even when we have experienced the forgiving love of God, we may have difficulty facing in its stark reality the fact that Jesus died for us. That he died for all human beings is accepted and affirmed, but the sticking point comes when I begin to recognize that I am no better than the people who either connived in or at least were too cowardly to try to prevent the death of Jesus. Dare I look into the eyes of Jesus as I imagine him hanging on the cross? What will I see in those eyes? I want to believe that Jesus died for me in the full knowledge of who I am, but I can also be afraid and sometimes even terrified to approach Jesus on the cross. Whatever the source of these fears—whether they arise from the reluctance to accept such love or from the apprehension that he will not be looking at me with love or from the thought that the acceptance of such love will bring on great demands —the fears are real enough and the exercise very difficult. Again it may take me time to let Jesus reveal that he still loves me even though I am one of the people who put him on the cross. The crucifixion is the ultimate consequence of our turning our backs on God's dream for us and our universe. If we can, by the grace of God, come to look Jesus in the eyes as he hangs on the cross and there find love, then we experience in a profound way the free and freeing unconditional love of God for us sinners. We will also have taken another step away from illusion and toward reality. We will know that we are indeed loved sinners and appreciate both the adjective and the noun. Moreover, in our hearts fear for ourselves will be subordinated to love for Jesus because we will know that nothing we have done or can do (except despair) can "separate us from the love of God that is in Christ Jesus our Lord" (Rom 8:39).

7

"Who Is My Neighbor?"

During the Vietnam War there was a peace conference at the University of Michigan. The small Jesuit community in which I lived invited some of the
participants to come over to our house for a beer after
the conference. When people arrived, I went out to the
kitchen to get beers and soft drinks for our guests. I was
not out of the living room more than five minutes, but
when I returned, I heard a man I deeply respected irately
saying to an equally angry foreign cleric, "Well, my
country, right or wrong!" It was an indication of how
inflamed discussions of that war could get. I am almost
certain that the man who said it did not fully believe the
words, but he blurted them out nonetheless. And he was
not quoting Cardinal Spellman. He was very angry at the
peace advocate who had so violently attacked the
United States for its role in Vietnam. Two men who
believed in and loved Jesus Christ were almost at blows
about a political issue. Was there some illusion at
work here?

John Macmurray, the Scottish philosopher mentioned earlier, throughout his life was concerned with
religion. But he wanted to distinguish real religion from
illusory religion. In fact, he maintained that religion, to
be real, had to concern itself with reality. His thinking
has had a strong influence on this book. I bring him up at
this point to tell the story of his experience in the First

World War. Within a few minutes of joining his unit in the trenches and while he and three mates were having tea and joking, a shell landed in the trench. The man around the corner was killed instantly and the man next to him at the corner was so badly wounded that he probably died. Macmurray says that this experience made death a reality for him, a part of life, and thus removed from him the fear of it. He also notes that the men on both sides of the trenches came to the conclusion that "war was simply stupidity, destruction, waste and futility." They "believed that our leaders were either rascals or blind leaders of the blind." On one occasion because of an injury he was back in England and was asked to preach in a church in full uniform. He took the occasion to advise these Christians to avoid a war mentality and hatred of the enemy. Instead they should stand aloof from the quarrel and thus be in a position "to undertake their proper task as Christians when the war was over, of reconciliation."

> The congregation took it badly; I could feel a cold hostility menacing me; and no one spoke to me when the service was over. It was after this service that I decided, on Christian grounds, that I should never, when the war was over, remain or become a member of any Christian church.

He notes that this resolve had no effect on his belief in Jesus Christ and that he always believed himself a Christian. However, this experience brought him to think "of the churches as the various national religions of Europe" (*Search for Reality in Religion*).

During the Vietnam War I had an experience somewhat similar to Macmurray's. I had been told that some Catholics would be passing out leaflets against the war after the masses at the parish I served. The gospel of the Sunday seemed to open itself to speaking of the responsibility we had as citizens of a democracy for the policies of our country. As Christians, I said, we had an obligation to reflect on what our country was about in Vietnam and to come to a responsible position on the war. To the best of my knowledge I did not advocate any position for or against the war. Yet at least one member of the congregation walked out during the homily, and a couple of others told me that I had no right to speak on the issue from the pulpit.

I do not mention these experiences to advocate a position on modern warfare. I mention them because I want to reflect on the issue raised by the expert in the law in Luke's gospel, "And who is my neighbor?" You recall the story. He wanted to test Jesus and asked him, "What must I do to inherit eternal life?" Jesus asked him, "What is written in the law? How do you read it?" " 'Love the Lord your God with all your heart and with all your soul and with all your strength and with all your mind'; and, 'Love your neighbor as yourself.' " Jesus responded, "You have answered correctly. Do this and you will live." To justify himself, then, the expert in the law put the question about his neighbor. In response to this question Jesus told the parable of the good Samaritan. As Robert Karris in the *New Jerome Biblical Commentary* (p. 702) notes, a priest and a levite, prime examples of law-abiding people, do not stop to help "the stripped and apparently dead man for fear of becoming defiled," but a pariah, a despised Samaritan, does. At the end of the parable Jesus asked, "Which of these three do you think was a neighbor to the man who fell into the hands of robbers?" In other words, Jesus says, "Don't ask who your neighbor is. Ask about the conduct required of someone who belongs to the people of God." The law expert answered, "The one who had mercy on him," to which Jesus said, "Go and do likewise." In effect, the parable says that a neighbor, and therefore a member of God's people, is anyone who helps those in need (Lk 10:25–37).

We often miss the emotional significance of the fact that the one who had mercy was a Samaritan. Once in Jamaica I heard a homily in which the story was told in Jamaican terms, and the Samaritan became a Rastafarian. The Rastafarians in Jamaica wear the "dreadlocks" (long ringlets of hair), use marijuana as a sacred herb, and believe that Haile Selassie is the reincarnation of Christ. At the time of the homily the Rastafarians were a rather feared and outcast group as far as most Christians were concerned. The point of the parable was rather strongly made. The feared Rastafarian who helps a person in need is a real Christian.

The story of the tower of Babel implies that the disunity of peoples symbolized and caused by the confusion of languages is the result of the pride and sin of human beings. Thus the original dream of God that people live in harmony as brothers and sisters is shattered by our refusal of God's dream for us, our belief that we could do for ourselves in this world. The story of Pentecost with the miracle of tongues implies that with Christ's resurrection and the coming of the Holy Spirit the disunity originating at the tower of Babel has been overcome in principle. The parable of the good Samaritan tells us that we are in tune with God's reality if we act as neighbor to anyone we meet who needs our help. No one is excluded from God's loving care.

Recently I heard a story attributed to a Jewish tradition. When the army of the Egyptians was destroyed by the Red Sea sweeping back over them, all those in heaven cheered and threw a party because the Israelites were saved. But they looked over and saw God weeping. They asked why he was weeping when his people had been saved and the Egyptians destroyed. God replied, "The Egyptians are my people too." That story speaks to the truth that all human beings are precious in God's eyes.

The stories with which we began this chapter indicate that many people do not accept this reality. In fact, throughout history, it seems, most people have not accepted this reality. Our own century has witnessed the horrors human beings can inflict on one another, often enough in the name of God. The Holocaust of the Jews and other undesirables in Nazi Germany was based on the premise that those slaughtered were a lower class of people. The Jim Crow laws and the racial prejudice of the United States relied and still rely on the same premise about Afro-Americans. At the present moment as the Russian empire begins to break up, we are seeing the reemergence of the embittered relations of peoples forced to live as though they were one country. Arabs and Jews in the Middle East are not acting as though they were brothers and sisters. Fear and hatred of those who are "different" from "us" seems to be endemic among human beings. Is it, then, a pipe dream to speak of God's desire as though it could be realized? Is it merely liberal idealism or pious rhetoric?

We have to look deeply into our hearts and ask ourselves how we want to live. Do we want to live with as much fear and dislike of others as we live with now? Are we content with the restrictions under which we live

because of the fear of others? Did we not feel a surge of
hope and desire evoked or remembered when we read
the first chapter? When we begin to doubt the possibility
of the dream, we are succumbing to the strategy Ignatius
ascribes to "the enemy of human nature." Because the
dream seems difficult, if not impossible, to achieve in
the real world, we fall back into the illusion that this is a
"dog eat dog" world and that security is only attained
from the barrel of a gun. But look where this illusion
leads us. We have the seemingly endless civil wars in
Lebanon, Northern Ireland, Afghanistan, Israel, the
countries of Central America, etc. The arms race between the United States and the Union of Soviet Social-
ist Republics has brought us to the point where the two
countries could annihilate one another thousands of
times over. The thought of ever using these arsenals
should send a shiver through any sane individual. The
strategy of Mutual Assured Destruction has an appropriate acronym. Is this realism?

Christians, and indeed all men and women, need to
ask God to convert us from the illusion that any human
being, just by belonging to a particular race or sex or
country, is an enemy to be feared. Every human being is
precious in God's eyes. Therefore every human being is,
at least potentially, my neighbor, my brother, my sister.
If I want to live realistically in this world, I must desire
to have my heart converted so that any human being,
from the unborn in the womb to the Alzheimer's patient
in the nursing home, from the peasant in China to my
next door neighbor, from Donald Trump to the pan-
handler just outside of Trump Plaza, is my neighbor. If
Christian churches are not places where prayers are regularly said not only for the soldiers of "our" country but
also for the "enemy" soldiers, not only for the victims of

rape but also for the rapists, not only for the unborn but also for those who ask for or perform abortions, then they may merit the same critique Macmurray made of the "Christian" churches of Europe during the First World War. He came to think of them as "the various national religions of Europe." The followers of Christ are asked to consider all human beings as at least potential brothers and sisters and to pray for them. We need to beg God to convert our hearts so that this is our attitude.

In Mark's gospel (7:24–30) Jesus is confronted by an alien, a Gentile woman who asks Jesus to use his healing power to drive out a demon from her daughter. Jews often called Gentiles "dogs." Jesus' reply to the woman's request seems to mirror that attitude. "First let the children eat all they want, for it is not right to take the children's bread and toss it to their dogs." Daniel Harrington in the *New Jerome Biblical Commentary* notes that the word here translated as "dogs" is better translated "puppies," and indicates that the use of the diminutive might have been a way of softening the offensive remark. Even if he is correct, it is an insult, and one that is not limited to Jews speaking of Gentiles. One of the readers of this manuscript told me of going into a Hindu temple in India and finding at the entrance of the inner holy place a sign that said, "Christians, Muslims and dogs forbidden!" However we interpret his remark, Jesus tells the woman that his healing power is reserved for Jews only. Her sick daughter is excluded from its radius. The woman replies with a witty remark, in effect telling Jesus that he is wrong in this exclusivity. "Yes, Lord, but even the dogs under the table eat the children's crumbs." Jesus says, "For such a reply, you may go; the demon has left your daughter." The gospel story's main focus is not on the healing but on the dialogue between

Jesus and the woman. The Gentile Christian readers of the gospel would know that they were included in the saving power of Jesus.

The starkness and seeming harshness of Jesus' initial response, however, invite us to speculate on whether Jesus here ran into a situation which shook up the categories which he, as any human being, learned from his culture. He knew that his mission to the Jewish people had a priority, that salvation would come from the Jews. Could it be that the encounter with this Syrophoenician woman brought about a conversion in him such that the priority remained, but the exclusiveness with which he had interpreted that priority for his own mission was seen to be illusory? It is no sin to be a product of one's culture even if the culture's exclusivity is objectively sinful in a world where God wants all people to be brothers and sisters. In this understanding of the text, Jesus is not converted from any personal sin, but from a cultural blindness. Through this Syrophoenician woman Jesus himself learns who is his neighbor. It is, indeed, a measure of his great-heartedness that he can learn from a Gentile. It may be a comforting thought as we struggle with our own tendencies to illusion to realize that Jesus can sympathize with us.

Another story from the New Testament may also comfort us and encourage us to trust those experiences that push us beyond our prejudices. In the early chapters of the Acts of the Apostles we get the impression that the first Christians still considered themselves believing Jews. Moreover, Jews treated them as an heretical sect of Judaism.

In chapter ten of Acts we read of the conversion of Cornelius, a centurion in the Roman army and a Gentile. Cornelius had a vision in which an angel told him to send for Peter, which he immediately did. The following day as Cornelius' messengers approached Joppa, Peter went up to pray. While his meal was being prepared, he fell into a trance. In the trance he saw a large sheet let down from heaven with all kinds of animals and reptiles on it. A voice said, "Get up, Peter. Kill and eat." Peter protested that he had never eaten unclean foods, thus indicating that he was still an observant Jew. This happened three times. While Peter was wondering what the dream meant, Cornelius' messengers arrived. The Spirit spoke to Peter, "Simon, three men are looking for you. So get up and go downstairs. Do not hesitate to go with them, for I have sent them." When Peter met the men, he invited them in to be his guests, although they were Gentiles, and the next day went with them to visit Cornelius. When they met, Peter told Cornelius, "You are well aware that it is against our law for a Jew to associate with a Gentile or visit him. But God has shown me that I should not call any man impure or unclean." Cornelius then explained what had happened to him, to which Peter replied, "I now realize how true it is that God does not show favoritism but accepts people from every nation who fear him and do what is right." Peter went on to preach the good news about Jesus, and while he was speaking, "the Holy Spirit came on all who heard the message." Peter ordered that they be baptized. Thus, through the grace of God Peter is converted from an exclusive view of who may be a follower of Christ to an inclusive one. No one is, in principle, excluded.

When the circumcised believers in Jerusalem heard what Peter had done, they criticized him saying, "You went into the house of uncircumcised men and ate with them." Peter then described his experiences and how the Holy Spirit came upon the house of Cornelius. "When they heard this, they had no further objections and praised God, saying, 'So then, God has granted even the Gentiles repentance unto life' " (Acts 10:1—11:18). It was very difficult for these first Christians to have their mindsets changed, but by the grace of God and their openness to the experience of God's action on them they were converted. We can, as I said earlier, take comfort from the difficulty which Jesus had with the Syrophoenician woman and which the first Christians had with allowing Gentiles into the fold and also trust that the dynamism of God's love at the heart of our universe will transform our hearts.

The following passage from the letter to the Hebrews speaks to that comfort:

> Therefore, since we have a great high priest who has gone through the heavens, Jesus the Son of God, let us hold firmly to the faith we profess. For we do not have a high priest who is unable to sympathize with our weaknesses, but we have one who has been tempted in every way, just as we are—yet was without sin. Let us then approach the throne of grace with confidence, so that we may receive mercy and find grace to help us in our time of need (Heb 4:14–16).

"Who is my neighbor?" Anyone who comes across my path, but also, at least in potential, any human being. John Donne's famous words provide a fitting conclusion to this chapter.

> No man is an island, entire of itself; every man is a piece of the continent, a part of the main; if a clod be washed away by the sea, Europe is the

less, as well as if a promontory were, . . . ; any man's death diminishes me, because I am involved in mankind; and therefore never send to know for whom the bell tolls; it tolls for thee. (*Devotions Upon Emergent Occasions*, no. 17.)

8

"Who Do You Say I Am?"

Chapter 4 was introduced by the story of the man possessed by the legion of demons. I want to bring him back to our attention here, but for another purpose.

> When Jesus got out of the boat, a man with an evil spirit came from the tombs to meet him. This man lived in the tombs, and no one could bind him any more, not even with a chain. For he had often been chained hand and foot, but he tore the chains apart and broke the irons on his feet. No one was strong enough to subdue him. Night and day among the tombs and in the hills he would cry out and cut himself with stones.
>
> When he saw Jesus from a distance, he ran and fell on his knees in front of him. He shouted at the top of his voice, "What do you want with me, Jesus, Son of the Most High God? Swear to God that you won't torture me!" (Mk 5:2–7)

Try to imagine yourself suddenly faced with this man. How would you feel? I know that when I come face to face with such rage and madness I feel threatened and frightened and want to run away. If I can do it decently, I do get away as quickly as possible. In fact, if I see such a person coming in my direction, I tend to quicken my steps and look for ways of avoiding any meeting at all. I am also relieved if I have company with me; at least I feel a bit protected. For a little while let yourself contemplate this gospel scene in your imagination and note your reactions.

How did Jesus react? He seemed to be calm and inwardly collected. He asked the man, "What is your name?" " 'My name is Legion,' he replied, 'for we are many.' And he begged Jesus again and again not to send them out of the area." Jesus' calm authority seems to have quieted this bedlam and reduced the crazed spirits to imploring him for a favor. Jesus obviously is a man in whom fear is subordinated to love. This crazed man whom most of us would try to avoid if we could and before whom most of us would find ourselves recoiling in fear brings out Jesus' interest and compassion. Moreover, Jesus even has compassion on the legion of evil spirits by letting them enter the herd of pigs. (The owners of the pigs probably wished that Jesus had had compassion on the pigs and them.) What kind of man is this? "Who do you say I am?" (Mt 16:15).

In Jesus' own day and throughout history men and women have been attracted to Jesus and wanted to find the answer to that question. For example, two disciples of John the Baptist heard John point to Jesus and say, "Look, the Lamb of God!" and "they followed Jesus. Turning around, Jesus saw them following and asked, 'What do you want?' They said, 'Rabbi' (which means Teacher), 'where are you staying?' 'Come,' he replied, 'and you will see' " (Jn 1:37–39). These two disciples and the many others who have followed Jesus in this way have desired to know him better, to know what makes him tick, what he values and loves. They are intrigued by him and want to become like him. Ignatius of Loyola in his Spiritual Exercises puts the desire of such people in this way: "Here it will be to ask for an intimate knowledge of our Lord, that I may love Him more and follow Him more closely" (no. 104). The desire is for intimate friendship with Jesus, and it ushers in a new phase of the process of conversion to the fullness of reality.

For the disciples of John the impetus to follow Jesus came from the words of John. For many Christians the desire to know Jesus more intimately arises after they have experienced the forgiving love of Jesus; for example, after they have looked into his eyes as he hangs on the cross and there found love. They want to get to know him better. If, however, they expect that the process of getting to know him better will be smooth sailing, they are in for a big surprise.

What do the first disciples discover about Jesus after the initial attraction that brings them into closer contact? Look at the first three chapters of Mark's gospel. The disciples are in the presence of a man with immense energy and intensity, a man of great compassion for the sick and suffering, a man who reaches out to the poor and the outcast, a man of prayer, a man from whom evil spirits recoil in horror, a man for whom people and their needs for compassion and love come before laws. He is wondrously attractive. But he also generates hostility in the leaders of his own religion and does not back down from controversy with them. The final straw for the religious leaders came when Jesus asked the man with a shriveled hand to stand up in the synagogue.

Then Jesus asked them (the Pharisees), "Which is lawful on the Sabbath: to do good or to do evil, to save life or to kill?" But they remained silent.

> He looked around at them in anger and,
> deeply distressed at their stubborn hearts, said
> to the man, "Stretch out your hand." He
> stretched it out, and his hand was completely
> restored. Then the Pharisees went out and be-
> gan to plot with the Herodians how they might
> kill Jesus (Mk 3:4–6).

Getting close to this man may be dangerous. Moreover,
it is possible that those who are close to him will be
excommunicated from the people of God.

Not only is Jesus unafraid of the rage of the crazed,
demon-possessed man and of the murderous jealousy
and fear of the Pharisees, but he also tells his followers
not to be afraid. In Matthew's gospel he sends out the
twelve disciples to carry out the same mission he has, to
preach the good news, drive out demons and heal the
sick. He tells them that they will suffer persecution for
his name's sake. The disciples had to know that they
were running the same risk Jesus ran. Jesus says, "When
they arrest you, do not worry about what to say or
how to say it" (Mt 10:19), and a little later in the dis-
course adds:

> So do not be afraid of them. There is nothing
> concealed that will not be disclosed, or hidden
> that will not be made known. What I tell you in
> the dark, speak in the daylight; what is whis-
> pered in your ear, proclaim from the roofs. Do
> not be afraid of those who kill the body but can-
> not kill the soul. Rather, be afraid of the One
> who can destroy both soul and body in hell. Are
> not two sparrows sold for a penny? Yet not one
> of them will fall to the ground apart from the
> will of your Father. And even the very hairs of

your head are all numbered. So don't be afraid;
you are worth more than many sparrows (Mt
10:26–31).

Following Jesus closely can indeed be dangerous.

These words of Jesus give us some clues as to how
Jesus himself came to be the kind of person he was. Obviously he has reflected on God's creative goodness and
providence in deep prayer. He believes that God cares
for the sparrows and the lilies of the field, that God loves
everything that God has made and keeps everything in
his care. Even persecution, suffering and death do not
change the reality of who God is and how God acts. The
gospels indicate that Jesus frequently went off by himself to pray, to commune with God. During the forty
days in the desert he must have marveled at the wonders
of nature and God's prodigal creativity and providence.
Jesus, the human being, let God and God's creative action or God's reign become the ruling love of his life.
Everything else, no matter how important, was second-
ary. Thus, health or sickness, a long life or a short one,
wealth or poverty, persecution or adulation, all took a
back seat to the ruling passion of his life, God and
God's reign.

Jesus, Christians believe, is the perfect human being, the one most in touch with God and with God's
intention for all persons. What we most deeply desire,
therefore, is to be like Jesus. What God most deeply desires is to make us like Jesus. In other words, the very
desire we have to know Jesus more intimately and become like him arises because God already wants the
same thing. If we could become like him, then we would
be fully in tune with the reality of this universe. We
would love the Lord our God with all our hearts and our

neighbor as ourselves. Our hearts would overflow with
the love of God, and all our fears would be subordinated
to this love. We would be the new persons de Rivera says
are needed if our world is to survive. What a wonderful dream!

But we know that the desire to know Jesus more
intimately in order to love him more and to follow him
more closely runs into some formidable roadblocks. The
rich young man (Mk 10:17–23) was attracted to Jesus
and wanted to know what he must do to inherit eternal
life. He has kept all the commandments all his life. "Jesus looked at him and loved him. 'One thing you lack,'
he said. 'Go, sell everything you have and give to the
poor, and you will have treasure in heaven. Then come,
follow me.' At this the man's face fell. He went away
sad, because he had great wealth." An inordinate attachment to something can become a source of resistance to
the desire to become like Jesus. In *Addiction and Grace*
Gerald May demonstrates how such attachments divert
us from the deepest desire of our hearts. The young man
in the gospel is addicted to his wealth, but the wealth
does not make him happy. He goes away sad. Jesus, who
"loved him," must have also been sad. We may be attached to our reputations, and the company Jesus keeps
may become a source of resistance to getting close to
him. Flannery O'Connor depicts the shock of the proper
"Christian" at the company Jesus keeps in the vision
Mrs. Turpin has of the bridge into heaven at the end of
the short story "Revelation."

> Upon it a vast horde of souls were rumbling
> toward heaven. There were whole companies of
> white-trash, clean for the first time in their
> lives, and bands of black niggers in white robes,

and battalions of freaks and lunatics shouting
and clapping and leaping like frogs. And bringing up the end of the procession was a tribe of
people whom she recognized at once as those
who, like herself and Claud, had always had a
little of everything and the God-given wit to
use it right. . . . They were marching behind the
others with great dignity, accountable as they
had always been for good order and common
sense and respectable behavior. They alone
were on key. Yet she could see by their shocked
and altered faces that even their virtues were
being burned away.

Jesus is obviously not interested in restricting his
friends to "our kind." Jesus' teaching may shake up
many of the values we live by, and we may feel the way
many of the disciples felt when they heard Jesus' words
about his own flesh as food. "This is a hard teaching.
Who can accept it?" (Jn 6:60).

The fears that cause resistance to intimate friendship with Jesus are more realistic fears than the fears
that we discussed earlier. In reality God is not the harsh
taskmaster the scrupulous person makes him out to be.
In reality no sinners, no matter how heinous the sins
they have committed, need fear to approach Jesus and
ask for forgiveness. But those who desire to become intimate friends of Jesus face realistic losses. The rich
young man faces the real loss of his money and what
money can buy. People who spend time with the out-
casts of society often find their reputations tarnished,
just as Jesus' reputation was tarnished. Tradition has it
that all but one of the twelve apostles died a martyr's
death. Through the centuries men and women who have

become imitators of Jesus—by grace, not by the efforts of their own will—have been persecuted, have suffered the loss of friends and reputation, have been put to death. These are not illusory losses. What is illusory, however, is the tendency to put fear of these losses before the deepest desire of our hearts, which is to be as much in tune with God's one creative action as possible, to live a life where fear is subordinated to love, to be a friend of Jesus, to be like Jesus. It is the inordinate attachment to wealth, reputation, family, health, and even life itself that is illusory because such attachments keep us from attaining what we most deeply desire. Insofar as these attachments rule our hearts we cannot live with fear subordinated to love; we will always be afraid of losing what we are attached to. Hence, they become more important than the desire to know Jesus intimately.

The important point here is the inordinate attachment, not the object of the attachment. Novices in the life of the spirit often believe that all they have to do to become like Christ is to give up everything they possess or are attached to. In J. F. Powers' novel *Wheat That Springeth Green,* Joe Hackett enters the seminary with the ambition of becoming a saint. He becomes the "spiritual" leader of a small group of seminarians who, after a retreat,

> in the quest of holiness, had gone into spiritual training, which had its physical side. "Detachment!" the retreatmaster had cried, and they gave up their attachments—smokes, sweets, snacks, snooker, and handball were Joe's—and haunted the chapel (pp. 41–42).

In the process Joe and his friends become prigs. Of

course, it does not last, thank God. Otherwise the novel would be unreadable, which it decidedly is not. Joe's inordinate attachment during his ascetic days is to the image of himself as a contemplative saint.

Ignatius of Loyola discovered the hard way that the issue of following Jesus is not one of giving up all that one has, but of allowing God to wean us away from our inordinate attachments. In his *Spiritual Exercises* he tells retreatants to beg God to give us the gift of spiritual poverty, which is the opposite of inordinate attachment, and even of actual poverty, *if* that is God's good pleasure. That is, we pray to have our inordinate attachments removed, but we leave it up to God whether we keep the object of our attachment or not. In the meditation on the three classes of persons, for example, he has retreatants consider people who have come into a large amount of money and now want to know what to do about the money. All three classes of persons who have the money want to do the will of God and live in peace but all are attached to the money. The first class talk a lot about what they should do and even make plans at times, but at the end of their life still have done nothing. The second class compromise; for example, they decide to keep the money and use part of it for charitable purposes. The third class do not do what Joe Hackett did; they do not give up the money immediately, but beg God to help them to decide whether to keep the money or give it up. In other words, they want God to decide how they should live their lives. They ask for detachment or spiritual poverty.

In point of fact our inordinate attachments to objects, reputation, health, friendships, life, etc. are so strong that they do function like addictions as Gerald May says. The harder we try on our own to control the addiction, the deeper we fall into its trap. If we want to be converted from the illusion these inordinate attachments represent, we must turn to a "higher Power," to the God whose passionate desire is for our freedom from fear and for our community with one another and with God. The wisdom of the Twelve-Step program is the wisdom all of the saints have learned, namely that we are helpless before our inordinate attachments and need the help of God to move beyond them to a happy, more fulfilled and challenging life. In order to become an intimate friend of Jesus we need the help of God to overcome our resistances.

The power of these resistances is nowhere more clearly seen than in our resistance to experiences that make us happy and give us what we most deeply desire, namely experiences of closeness to God. I have written about this strange type of resistance in three chapters of *Paying Attention to God.* Among other instances I described resistance to the desire to get close to Jesus or to love as Jesus loves. One of the illusions that can get in the way of really knowing Jesus is the notion that Jesus had to content himself with the love of God alone. Thus, if I am to love as Jesus loves, I must be willing to love without any return. What looms before me, then, is a pretty bleak life in which I give to others all the time and get nothing in return. Who would not resist such a life? The illusion consists in not recognizing that Jesus, in fact, did have friends and still has friends. What is true is that Jesus' love for his friends was not conditioned on their reciprocation; what is false is that Jesus had no friends. What I need to ask for is the grace to become a person in whom love, not fear, is the dominant motive. I cannot attain this position by my own willpower. However, I will also resist asking for this grace because of the consequences of getting it. After all, if I do become like Jesus, I will have to give over control of everything in my life to God. Even though all that I would be doing in this instance is acknowledging reality, it seems more than anyone can be asked to do. Something deep within us still responds to the siren call of the serpent in the garden, " 'You will not surely die,' the serpent said to the woman. 'For God knows that when you eat of it your eyes will be opened, and you will be like God, knowing good and evil' " (Gen 3:4–5). As Frost could say, "Something there is that does not like a fence," something within each of us there is that does not like any God but ourselves. Until we are converted from this illusion, we will never have the peace that surpasses all understanding nor will we ever have hearts where fear is subordinated to love, hearts like the heart of Christ.

Earlier I noted that John Macmurray was concerned with real religion. I want to end this chapter with an aphorism of his which bears much reflection.

> All religion . . . is concerned to overcome fear. We can distinguish real religion from unreal by contrasting their formulae for dealing with negative motivation. The maxim of illusory religion runs: "Fear not; trust in God and He will see that none of the things you fear will happen to you"; that of real religion, on the contrary, is "Fear not; the things that you are afraid of are quite likely to happen to you, but they are nothing to be afraid of."

9

The Call to Discipleship

In the synoptic gospels Jesus three times predicts his passion and death. Each time the twelve disciples miss the point. In Mark the first prediction occurs right after Peter has confessed, "You are the Christ." Jesus spoke plainly about his coming passion and death, but Peter, the man who had just spoken with such insight, "took him aside and began to rebuke him" (Mk 8:27–33). It is not clear from the gospel why Peter was so vehement. Possibly he cannot believe that Jesus' mission will not succeed in the only way Peter can measure success, victory for their side. After the second prediction the evangelist writes, "But they did not understand what he meant and were afraid to ask him about it" (Mk 9:30–32). The disciples then went on to argue with one another "about who was the greatest" (34). "Sitting down, Jesus called the Twelve and said, 'If anyone wants to be first, he must be the very last, and the servant of all' " (35). Discipleship, it seems, means the reversal of the usual value systems by which people live their lives. After the third prediction (Mk 10:32–34) James and John came to Jesus and asked if they could sit at his right and left in his glory. When the other disciples

> . . . heard about this, they became indignant
> with James and John. Jesus called them together
> and said, "You know that those who are re-

garded as rulers of the Gentiles lord it over them, and their high officials exercise authority over them. Not so with you. Instead, whoever wants to become great among you must be your servant, and whoever wants to be first must be slave of all. For even the Son of Man did not come to be served, but to serve, and to give his life as a ransom for many" (10:41–45).

Obviously the disciples are depicted as very resistant to getting the point of Jesus' message. In the last chapter I pointed out that one source of the resistance to getting close to Jesus could be the fear of the consequences. I want to use the story of the disciples to point out yet another possible source of resistance. The disciples seem unable to imagine not succeeding, almost as though they say to themselves, "Jesus' cause, which we have embraced, is right. Sure, we will have difficulties, but it must succeed."

Another scene in the gospels shows a similar attitude. On his way to Jerusalem Jesus was not welcomed into a Samaritan village. "When the disciples James and John saw this, they asked, 'Lord, do you want us to call fire down from heaven to destroy them?' But Jesus turned and rebuked them" (Lk 9:54–55). If they do not succeed in their mission, then anger blazes up in the disciples and they want to destroy the village. We can discern whether we are motivated by love for others in our actions by noticing how we react when they are not grateful for what we have done for them or do not accept our action.

As I write this chapter, I am reminded of a front page story in today's *Boston Globe* (July 16, 1990). Last week Mitch Snyder, the most visible advocate for the homeless in the United States, committed suicide. Many felt a deep sense of loss. The article discusses the troubled lives of many social activists like Mitch Snyder. The writer notes, "Activists frequently neglect their personal lives to devote extra energy to their causes, leaving a trail of broken marriages and relationships." Such activists exhibit vast reservoirs of energy and passion for their causes and attract others to join. It is a heady life. But the cause, it seems, can become all-consuming. Friends of Mitch Snyder, for example, say that nothing else mattered to him but the plight of the homeless and that he judged people solely on how much they did for the homeless. His own words of self-description placed at the end of the article are telling.

> I don't consider myself a good person. I tend to be very impatient, I tend to be very short, I tend to make heavy demands on people. I don't have time or energy to give much one-on-one, and so I'm hard on the people around me. I take much more than I give. I give to people in the shelter, I give to people on the streets, I give to people who are suffering, but that's got little to do with people who are around me. They pay the price.

As I read this sad article about Mitch Snyder and other activists, I had the thought that they might be addicted to the success of their cause, and so suffer great bouts of depression when it becomes clear not only that they are not succeeding but that the enthusiasm for the cause among their supporters is waning. Obviously, given the tremendous self-giving and genuine charity of many activists, it would be terribly wrong to discount their actions by such an analysis. I do not bring up this article to point the finger at anyone. I believe that every one of us needs to examine our experience to see where God is asking conversion of us. After I look at the issue of addiction to the success of the mission, I will invite us to look at another illusion; namely that we are powerless to effect any change in unjust social structures.

Jesus, obviously, had no illusions about the "success" of his mission. He could sense the storm clouds growing more ominous; he felt the rising hatred and fear of the leaders of the Jewish people. He wanted to let the disciples know what he and they were in for, but they were blind to his predictions, perhaps because of the illusion that his cause could not but succeed. The crowds were with them, were they not? But Jesus was not taken in by adulation. In John's gospel we read:

> Now while he was in Jerusalem at the Passover Feast, many people saw the miraculous signs he was doing and believed in his name. But Jesus would not entrust himself to them, for he knew all men. He did not need man's testimony about man, for he knew what was in a man (Jn 2:23–25).

Jesus was not addicted to "success." He clearly knew the reality of our world; namely that our only real happiness lies in union with God and that nothing else, not even the conversion of the whole world, can satisfy us if we do not have that union. The temptations in the desert put before him the temptations all human beings face (Mt 4:1–11). In his hunger after forty days of fasting he heard the words, "If you are the Son of God, tell these stones to become bread." Will he use his power not only to assuage his hunger but also to prove himself? Or will he put his trust in God? Jesus quoted Deuteronomy, "It is written: 'Man does not live on bread alone, but on every word that comes from the mouth of God.' " Secondly Jesus was tempted to a rash trust in God. The devil took him to the temple's pinnacle and said, "If you are the Son of God, throw yourself down. For it is written: 'He will command his angels concerning you, and they will lift you up in their hands, so that you will not strike your foot against a stone.' " Will Jesus unnecessarily risk his life in a foolish effort to prove to himself and to others that he is the Son of God? Again Jesus quoted Deuteronomy, "It is also written, 'Do not put the Lord your God to the test.' " Finally the devil promised Jesus all the power and wealth of the world if only he will worship the devil. And Jesus made the final assertion of his faith, "Away from me, Satan! For it is written, 'Worship the Lord your God, and serve him only.' " In other words, Jesus' only final commitment was to God. He trusted finally only in God, and not in power or wealth or even in the "success" of his mission. Jesus put his ultimate trust in his Father and in no one or nothing else.

Mind you, it may not have been easy for Jesus. The fact that the gospels speak of "temptations" means that they must have had some attraction for Jesus. After all, as we have seen in another instance, Jesus is a product of his culture just as every human being is. The "just world hypothesis" was as much a part of his world as it is of ours. But he transcended his culture through his experience of God and in this way became free of the illusions all human beings are prone to. Still the agony in the garden indicates that even Jesus had to face the ultimate test of his faith and trust in God. Will he "go gently into that good night," the night of the total failure of his mission, trusting that God would still come through not only for him, but also for God's people? The depth of the agony is conveyed by the triple prayer to God (in Mark and Matthew), by the fact that he seems to seek consolation from his disciples (again in Mark and Matthew) and by the sweat of blood (in Luke). The final agony on the cross faces us with those terrible words, "My God, my God, why have you forsaken me?" recorded in both Mark and Matthew. The ultimate test of his trust in God seems to wrack Jesus. Moreover, these two gospels do not provide any softening of these words. In both we hear that Jesus let out a loud cry and breathed his last. John's gospel is a bit more comforting to those who contemplate the scene of the crucifixion. "With that, he bowed his head and gave up his spirit." Only in Luke do we hear the words of surrender, "Father, into your hands I commit my spirit." Jesus faced the shipwreck of his whole life in a degrading, horrible death, betrayed, denied or abandoned by his closest friends. Throughout his life he had relied on the reality of God's call to him and to all of us to put our ultimate trust only in God. Now he faced the final test of that trust, and he came through it still trusting in God.

Those of us who follow Jesus with passion need to contemplate in depth Jesus' own life and death and to beg God to give us hearts like the heart of Jesus. We are so prone to illusion, to making idols of even our own good causes and intentions. Once again, I want to return to the wisdom of Ignatius of Loyola. As we saw in the last chapter, he counseled people who wanted to become intimate friends of Jesus not to choose their own ways of following Jesus. It is not a virtue to choose actual poverty with Christ poor if God does not want me to live that way. It is not a virtue to choose to live a celibate life if God does not choose me for that life. I can become so enamored of the image of myself as the "heroic follower of Christ" that the image becomes an illusion. Often enough men and women of immense good will and enthusiasm have chosen their own ways of life and attributed the choice to a "vocation" only to cause great harm to their own health and lives and to those who are close to them. Conversion to the God of this real world means to become converted to the reality of Jesus and to his way. In *The Practice of Spiritual Direction* William Connolly and I tried to spell out what such a conversion might mean.

> This experience of Jesus shows itself in an ability to live by one's own convictions despite other people's opposition to those convictions; in a breadth of empathy that transcends social and economic class; in a deepening trust of the Father of reality; in a willingness to engage in the war against evil and to stand for justice and mercy even when one must die small deaths in defense of them; and a willingness to die those deaths and leave resurrection to the Father (p. 112).

Here I might add that the experience shows itself also in the ability to love even those who thwart one's cause and seem to be one's enemies.

Once again we need to remind ourselves that will-power alone will not give us these qualities. The only way to become like Jesus is to contemplate his life, to ask him to reveal himself to us so that we can love him more and follow him more closely. We become like the people whom we get to know intimately and to love. The process of becoming like another happens almost by osmosis. Because we love Jesus, we admire his values and ask to share them. We beg him and God to give us hearts like the heart of Christ so that we value what he values. These values do not easily take over our hearts because we are caught up in the illusions fostered by our culture, but also in the illusion that seems to have been with us since the dawn of human time, namely that we can control our own lives and deaths. Such illusions die hard and can only be overcome by the grace of God for which we must earnestly pray.

Jesus found himself faced with a formidable set of adversaries, and he had very few resources with which to confront them. The political and religious establishment were arrayed against this layman with no political base. He did not see his role to be that of a revolutionary leader who would galvanize the people to throw off their shackles in an armed struggle. He seems to have seen himself as a religious leader who had an urgent message to preach, namely the imminent inbreak of the reign of God. It is rather startling to realize that such a message could bring down on him the malice of both the political and religious establishment. To take God seriously and to preach God's dream for our world is, obviously, a dangerous business. It threatens established institutions.

It is easy to trivialize the gospel call. For years people were taught that Jesus chose suffering, humiliation and death and that discipleship meant that they, too, choose the same things. So they chose to make "fools" of themselves by decisions to do menial tasks such as washing toilet bowls or to look unkempt by not washing or taking care of their hair or finger nails. But the gospel call is to live in freedom from illusions, to question assumptions that cripple our imaginations and our lives and imprison us in fear, to challenge injustice whereever it may be found. To be a fool for Christ's sake means to risk being honest in a world where dishonesty seems in favor, being courageous where caution is a way of life. Those who choose to follow Jesus will suffer some dying, but death is not what they choose.

Ultimately the contemplation of Jesus faces us with the choice of whether we are ready to follow Jesus even though it may mean death or diminishment at the hands of those who are imprisoned and made violent by their own fears and assumptions. Jesus was killed by men, but they would not have killed him if they had not been imprisoned in a system or social structure that they believed was necessary, even sacred. Against such powers of "this world" the only "weapon" Jesus had was the truth. Pilate's cynical remark, "What is truth?" (Jn 18:38) has been echoed by other tyrants through the ages. Joseph Stalin is supposed to have asked, "How many divisions does the Pope have?" Against these powers the success of the truth does not often come in the magical way we hope. The cross is the Christian symbol of success. When we can embrace the cross for ourselves, then the illusion of "success" has been broken.

Because the cross is the symbol of Christian success, many people can be lulled into another illusion, namely that God is not interested in what happens in the social and political arena. Because the institutions of our world, such as governments, corporations and churches, are so massive, we can take a passive stance toward the unjust situations these institutions sometimes lead to or foster. The attitude that "You can't fight City Hall" takes over, and we retreat to a privatized religion where the only morality is a personal one. God's desire then seems to become that I live as good a life as I can in the circumstances of my life without being concerned about the injustices around me. That I am living an illusion becomes apparent if I look honestly at Jesus' life. No one would have wanted to kill him if he had taken the tack in life I am tempted to take. The God Jesus preached was and is a threat to the powers that be, precisely because the reign of God is both immanent in as well as transcendent to this world. Hence, those who believe in Jesus' God believe that the institutions of this world must be so constructed that they help people to live out God's dream. The God of Jesus wants his people to love and care for one another and not be consumed by fears for themselves. In a world becoming increasingly a "global village" because of modern means of communication my neighbor can be a peasant in El Salvador or a political prisoner in China, and to help that neighbor I may need to take public stands that are unpopular. If, as we contended in chapter 2, hope for a just and harmonious world is not illusory, then the disciples of Jesus are called to be part of the movement toward that end. To be in tune with God's intention for this world means to work together with others to make the structures and institutions of this world more in tune with God's intentions. Real religion is not the opium of the people.

10

It Was Not a Bad Dream

In a moving letter to a woman whose husband had left her (cited by Monica Furlong), Thomas Merton wrote:

> I know from my own experience that the loneliness and confrontation with death only become intolerable when I have unconsciously argued myself into a position in which I am in fact refusing to accept them and insisting that there is some other way. But there is no other way . . . I wonder if you are not doing what so many of us do: acting on the assumption that one ought not to be lonely and that one ought not to be travelling towards death, in fact that one ought not to be tempted to faithlessness and despair.

The human tendency before the threat of suffering and death is to hope that it is all a bad dream.

The disciples of Jesus had put all their hopes on Jesus and the success of his mission. In the last chapter we noted that they could not seem to hear Jesus when he predicted his suffering and death. When he was so cruelly and mercilessly tortured and killed, all their hopes were dashed. With the resurrection appearances they could have been tempted to believe that the crucifixion along with their own cowardice was just a bad dream.

But the risen Jesus carries the wounds of the passion. It was not a bad dream. In fact, only by accepting the reality of the passion and crucifixion with all the attendant circumstances that might arouse their shame can the disciples have the joy of the resurrection. To the extent that the fear of looking directly at the suffering and death of Jesus controls their minds and hearts, to that extent they miss the joy of Jesus' resurrection. The joy of the resurrection means, as Sebastian Moore states, that "(l)ife is no longer lived under the shadow of death, it is in the light with death behind us. The virus of eternity has entered our bloodstream for ever" (*Jesus the Liberator of Desire*, p. 57). But if the disciples do not, in their bones, know that Jesus died horribly and that they in their cowardice did nothing to stop it, then they are not living "in the light with death behind us."

The fact that they did accept the full reality of Jesus' cross is proved by the way they lived after Pentecost. Not only did these formerly fearful and cowardly men preach openly and without fear, but they also rejoiced when they suffered for Christ's sake. After they were flogged by the Sanhedrin, they left "rejoicing because they had been counted worthy of suffering disgrace for the Name. Day after day, in the temple courts and from house to house, they never stopped teaching and proclaiming the good news that Jesus is the Christ" (Acts 5:41–42). It appears that fear of suffering and death no longer has a stranglehold on them. They who once were half alive because of their fears are now fully alive in Christ, and not even the spectre of persecution and death can take away their joy. They have chosen life to the fullest, have looked reality in the eye, and live "in the light with death behind" them.

Is it possible for ordinary mortals like ourselves to come to such a state of conversion to reality? In chapter 2 I mentioned that John Macmurray had faced death in the trenches of France in World War I and said that he no longer had any fear of death. In our own day we have many examples of ordinary people like ourselves who were not so crippled by their fear of death that they could not speak the truth. Archbishop Oscar Romero of El Salvador is one example. By God's grace he was transformed from a rather timid intellectual seminary professor into a bishop who so threatened the powers that be in his country that they had him killed. The many catechists among the poor people of Latin America who kept on with their teaching in spite of threats of torture and death and who eventually suffered both are another example. The Blacks and Whites who joined together to protest segregation in a nonviolent way in the United States in the sixties are another. The masses of people in the Philippines who stood before armed troops and tanks to protest against what they saw as a stolen election are another. There are many more. In chapter 2 I mentioned Etty Hillesum, the Dutch Jewess who died in Auschwitz. Here is a modern day example of how a real relationship with God can transform a person.

We have her diary entries for the two-year period 1941 to 1943, published under the title *An Interrupted Life.* Etty was born on January 15, 1914, one of three brilliant children of the turbulent marriage between a Dutch Jewish schoolteacher and headmaster and a Russian Jewish mother. After leaving her father's school in 1932, Etty took her first degree in law at the University of Amsterdam and then enrolled in the department of Slavonic Languages. The diaries indicate that she earned some of her living expenses by tutoring in Russian. We do not know much of her life up to Sunday, March 9, 1941, when she made her first entry in her diaries.

From the diaries we learn that her life revolved around two circles of people, one the group of five with whom she lived, the other a group of followers of a somewhat enigmatic and yet mesmerizing German Jew, Julius Spier. The group of five was headed by a 62 year old widower, Han Wegerif who had invited Etty in as a sort of housekeeper. She soon became his lover. Etty met Spier in January, 1941, it seems, and soon became his patient in a rather strange psychotherapy that included wrestling. After a few sessions she became his confidant and then his lover. Psychologists could have a field day analyzing Etty's transference and Spier's countertransference. Yet through this relationship Etty found God. After Spier died in September, 1942, Etty addresses him in her diary: "You taught me to speak the name of God without embarrassment. You were the mediator between God and me, and now you, the mediator, have gone and my path leads straight to God. It is right that it should be so. And I shall be the mediator for any other soul I can reach" (pp. 209–10).

Near the end of the diaries after Spier's death, Etty writes:

> And when the turmoil becomes too great and I am completely at my wits' end, then I still have my folded hands and bended knee. A posture that is not handed down from generation to generation with us Jews. I have had to learn it the hard way. It is my most precious inheritance from the man whose name I have almost forgotten but whose best part has become a constit-

uent of my own life. What a strange story it really is, my story: the girl who could not kneel. Or its variation: the girl who learned to pray. That is my most intimate gesture, more intimate even than being with a man. After all one can't pour the whole of one's love out over a single man, can one?" (p. 240).

Whatever else we can say about the therapeutic relationship between Etty and Spier—and Etty was not blind to Spier's weaknesses—he was the catalyst for a remarkable transformation in Etty Hillesum. In the course of the year and a half recorded in these diaries Etty develops from a young woman controlled by her moods and fears to a spiritually mature person who can fairly be described as a mystic in the hell created by the Nazis in occupied Europe. And it happened because she took the relationship with God seriously.

Her diaries testify both to what the relationship with God can do and to what it cannot do. About a year after she had begun to address God "without embarrassment" she wrote: "We try to save so much in life with a vague sort of mysticism. Mysticism must rest on crystal-clear honesty, can only come after things have been stripped down to their naked reality" (p. 149). What she meant by this crystal-clear honesty becomes clarified a couple of months later in this entry.

Something has crystallized. I have looked our destruction, our miserable end which has already begun in so many small ways in our daily life, straight in the eye and accepted it into my life, and my love of life has not been diminished. I am not bitter or rebellious, or in any

> way discouraged. . . . I have come to terms with
> life. . . . By "coming to terms with life" I mean:
> the reality of death has become a definite part
> of my life; my life has, so to speak, been ex-
> tended by death, by my looking death in the eye
> and accepting it, by accepting destruction as
> part of life and no longer wasting my energies
> on fear of death or the refusal to acknowledge
> its inevitability. It sounds paradoxical: by ex-
> cluding death from our life we cannot live a full
> life, and by admitting death into our life we en-
> large and enrich it (pp. 162–63).

We can paraphrase her paradox this way: by excluding
God from our life we cannot live a full life, and by admitting God into our life we enlarge and enrich it. For
Etty came to realize that admitting God into her life
meant to admit not only death but also all the suffering
of the world.

She quavered before the consequences of this kind
of crystal-clear honesty, but even then she could tell
God her fears as well. Take this entry a few days after
the last one cited. "Dear God, these are anxious times.
Tonight for the first time I lay in the dark with burning
eyes as scene after scene of human suffering passed before me." Could it not be that Etty, in her new-found
closeness to God, was seeing the world as God sees it
and feeling God's pathos in the process? She goes on:

> I shall promise You one thing, God, just one
> very small thing: I shall never burden my today
> with cares about my tomorrow, although that
> takes some practice. Each day is sufficient unto
> itself. I shall try to help You, God, to stop my

strength ebbing away, though I cannot vouch
for it in advance. But one thing is becoming increasingly clear to me: that You cannot help us,
that we must help You to help ourselves.

Here, it seems to me, Etty is experiencing the helplessness of God to change human hearts. In some people the
experience of God's helplessness rouses anger. God
seems useless to them. Etty, however, goes on:

And that is all we can manage these days and
also all that really matters: that we safeguard
that little piece of You, God, in ourselves. And
perhaps in others as well. Alas, there doesn't
seem to be much You Yourself can do about our
circumstances, about our lives. Neither do I
hold You responsible. You cannot help us but
we must help You and defend Your dwelling
place inside us to the last. . . . . . no one is in
their (the Nazis') clutches who is in Your arms. I
am beginning to feel a little more peaceful,
God, thanks to this conversation (p. 186–87).

Etty has realized that God cannot change the situation of
the Jews in Europe. Perhaps at first she reacted with
anger; the diaries do not tell us this. One thing is clear
from the diaries: closeness to God does not diminish
pain; it may even enhance it because one experiences
God's pain. Etty has not run away from God's pain and
ends up "a little more peaceful."

Lest it seem that closeness to God leads to nothing
but pain and suffering, let us look a bit further in this
same prayer. She recalls the jasmine tree behind her

house which has been destroyed by storms and then goes on to say to God:

> But somewhere inside me the jasmine continues to blossom undisturbed, just as profusely and delicately as ever it did. And it spreads its scent round the House in which You dwell, oh God. You can see, I look after You, I bring You not only my tears and my forebodings on this stormy, grey Sunday morning, I even bring you scented jasmine. And I shall bring You all the flowers I shall meet on my way, and truly there are many of those. I shall try to make You at home always. Even if I should be locked up in a narrow cell and a cloud should drift past my small barred window, then I shall bring You that cloud, oh God, while there is still the strength in me to do so. I cannot promise You anything for tomorrow, but my intentions are good, You can see (p. 188).

A measure of her inner happiness in spite of the horrors around her can be seen in the postcard she threw out of the window of the train transporting her and many others to certain death in Auschwitz. On it she had written: "We have left the camp singing." Apparently she found it true to the end that life is enlarged and enriched by the paradoxical act of accepting death (and God) into it. We cannot share the joy of Jesus' resurrection unless we are enabled to share the reality of his passion and death.

Moreover, the more in communion with God she becomes, the more open she is to suffering humanity. In September of 1942 she writes of her desires:

With a sharp pang, all of suffering mankind's nocturnal distress and loneliness passes now through my small heart. What shall I be taking upon myself this winter?
"One day, I would love to travel through all the world, oh God; I feel drawn right across all frontiers and feel a bond with all Your warring creatures." And I would like to proclaim that bond in a small, still voice but also compellingly and without pause. But first I must be present on every battle-front and at the centre of all human suffering (p. 225).

Her diaries end with these words, "We should be willing to act as a balm for all wounds." Apparently Etty was willing.

This diary is an extraordinary testimony to the possibilities of living without illusions in this world. In addition, it proves the wisdom of Merton's letter to the woman whose husband had abandoned her. The only way to enjoy life, to live life is to face suffering and death squarely. Etty's willingness to be "a balm for all wounds" finds an echo in another testimony from the horrors of the Holocaust. The soldiers who liberated a death camp found a prayer written on a piece of wrapping paper near the body of a dead child.

O Lord,
remember not only the men and women of
    goodwill
but also those of ill will.
But do not remember the suffering they have
    inflicted on us.

Remember the fruits we brought to this
    suffering,
our comradeship, our loyalty, our humility,
the courage, the generosity,
the greatness of heart which has grown out of
    all this.
And when they come to judgement,
let all the fruits that we have borne be their
    forgiveness. Amen.
(Cited in Alan Jones, *Passion for Pilgrimage*.)

We can end this chapter with Jesus' words to his
disciples, wisdom that came from his own experience of
looking at life through the eyes of God.

Therefore I tell you, do not worry about your
life, what you will eat; or about your body,
what you will wear. Life is more than food, and
the body more than clothes. Consider the ra-
vens: They do not sow or reap, they have no
storeroom or barn; yet God feeds them. And
how much more valuable you are than birds!
Who of you by worrying can add a single hour
to his life? Since you cannot do this very little
thing, why do you worry about the rest?
Consider how the lilies grow. They do not labor
or spin. Yet I tell you, not even Solomon in all
his splendor was dressed like one of these. If
that is how God clothes the grass of the field,
which is here today, and tomorrow is thrown
into the fire, how much more will he clothe
you, O you of little faith! And do not set your
heart on what you will eat or drink; do not
worry about it. For the pagan world runs after

all such things, and your Father knows that you need them. But seek his kingdom, and these things will be given to you as well.

Do not be afraid, little flock, for your Father has been pleased to give you the kingdom. Sell your possessions and give to the poor. Provide purses for yourselves that will not wear out, a treasure in heaven that will not be exhausted, where no thief comes near and no moth destroys. For where your treasure is, there your heart will be also (Lk 12:22–34).

11

"Converted Every Day"

A friend of mine told me of a couple of discussions with a woman who is a paraplegic unable to talk as a result of an accident. She communicates by pointing to letters on a letter board. One day she wanted to talk about prayer. Pointing to letters she told my friend that she kept saying the Our Father and the Hail Mary over and over. He asked her about the experience. She said that she felt a sense of being cared for, of being protected; she felt safe. Some days later she beckoned him into her room at the nursing home and pointed out this sentence, "He wants us to be converted every day." What insight she has been given! Given our capacity for illusion we do need to be converted every day, and many times every day at that. In his masterly study *Christian Conversion* Walter Conn gives this definition.

> Christian religious conversion is a fundamental shift from the instinctive but illusory assumption of absolute autonomy, the spontaneously defensive posture of radical, self-sufficient egocentrism, to the reflective openness and personal commitment of love in total surrender of self to God. The realistic recognition that one's

very being is a gift of love prompts the loving gift of one's entire life (p. 258).

Such a conversion cannot be a once for all event, I believe. We do need to be converted every day.

Perhaps the last illusion that keeps us from full surrender to God is the temptation to rely on our own goodness or on our membership in a particular organization as a guarantee of our salvation and safety.

> To some who were confident of their own righteousness and looked down on everybody else, Jesus told this parable: "Two men went up to the temple to pray, one a Pharisee and the other a tax collector. The Pharisee stood up and prayed about himself: 'God, I thank you that I am not like other men—robbers, evildoers, adulterers—or even like this tax collector. I fast twice a week and give a tenth of all I get.'
>
> "But the tax collector stood at a distance. He would not even look up to heaven, but beat his breast and said, 'God, have mercy on me, a sinner.'
>
> "I tell you that this man, rather than the other, went home justified before God. For everyone who exalts himself will be humbled, and he who humbles himself will be exalted" (Lk 18:9-14).

But even the tax collector can now become proud, as a reenactment of the story in which I participated in Brazil showed. As the Pharisee and tax collector left the temple, the tax collector was very happy and exultant because he had been justified, while the Pharisee was glum and sad at the judgment made on him. The next day the two came to the temple again. As they approached, the tax collector was jubilant and proud of himself and began to look down on the Pharisee who walked bowed down and puzzled. The tax collector's prayer became a mirror of the Pharisee's of the day before, while the Pharisee asked God why he had been so harshly judged. Eventually both have to learn that salvation comes only as a free gift of God. No one can boast of having earned it, and no one is "better" because of his or her works.

A version of the same illusion relies on doing a particular religious practice or on belonging to a particular organization. Many of us "made" the nine First Fridays, going to mass and receiving communion on the first Friday of each month for nine consecutive months in honor of the Sacred Heart of Jesus. We were told that if we did the practice we were assured of final penitence, thus having a guarantee of salvation. Insofar as we practiced this devotion in order to have the guarantee, we were living an illusion. God is always active in this world to bring everyone into union with him. No single practice of ours makes God more active or more merciful. Of course, devotion to the Sacred Heart of Jesus in itself is not an illusion; in fact, it is a recognition of the reality that Jesus died for love of us sinners and that that love is our only guarantee of salvation. There has been a persistent tradition that no one who died as a member of the Society of Jesus would go to hell. Again, if anyone joined the Society or remained a member for the guarantee of salvation, he would be putting his trust in this "work" and not in the God of love. Our desire for a guarantee of salvation comes from the persistent illusion that we can control our own destiny. That illusion dies very hard. Hence, God "wants us to be converted every day."

We cannot be our own master. Indeed the illusion that tries to tell us that we can leads us to becoming unfree. In *New Seeds of Contemplation* Thomas Merton says:

> (A)s long as you pretend to live in pure autonomy, as your own master, without even a god to rule you, you will inevitably live as the servant of another man or as the alienated member of an organization. Paradoxically, it is the acceptance of God that makes you free and delivers you from human tyranny (p. 110).

We can only be free if we surrender ourselves to God. We can only enjoy life if we surrender our illusion of control over it to God. We can only enjoy our friends if we surrender them to God. To the extent that we are gripped by the illusion that we can control our own destinies, to that extent fear for ourselves predominates over love for others and God, and when fear predominates, we are not free.

In the garden of Eden Adam and Eve ate the fruit of the forbidden tree because the serpent had promised that they would become like God. In reality, if we would be like God, there is only one thing that we can do to attain that desire: beg God to make our hearts like the heart of Jesus and contemplate Jesus as he appears in the gospels. Jesus, of all human beings, had a heart where love for others predominated over any fear for himself. As a result he was a supremely free man. Our world desperately needs people like him. As I was writing this

chapter, I came upon these words of John Barton in
Love Unknown, cited in a review in *The Tablet* for
July 7, 1990.

> God freely embraced the lot of the whole hu-
> man race, including—above all—its helpless-
> ness and bondage to death and suffering. That is
> the kind of God . . . who will "break his own
> heart to comfort ours," and who offers us the
> chance to become people who will do the same
> for each other and, indeed, for the least of our
> brothers and sisters.

The conversion process described in this book is God's
offer of that chance, the chance to attain the deepest
desire of our hearts and to be part of God's one action
which is his reign. "Now choose life" (Dt 30:19).

Annotated Bibliography

Barry, William A. *God and You: Prayer as a Personal Relationship.* Mahwah, NJ: Paulist, 1987.

———. *"Seek My Face": Prayer as Personal Relationship in Scripture.* Mahwah, NJ: Paulist, 1989.

———. *Paying Attention to God: Discernment in Prayer.* Notre Dame, IN: Ave Maria, 1990.

Berry, Thomas. *The Dream of the Earth.* San Francisco: Sierra Club Books, 1988. I have only fleetingly mentioned the need to be converted to the reality of our dependence on the environment. Berry explores this reality with an urgency that needs to energize us all.

Buechner, Frederick. *Godric.* San Francisco: Harper & Row, 1980. A wonderful novel about the life of a twelfth-century English holy man and his struggles with conversion.

Carmody, Denise. *Seizing the Apple: A Feminist Spirituality of Spiritual Growth.* New York: Crossroad, 1984. I have not adverted to the need for most men to be converted from our illusions about women. This well-written book describes the theory and practice of a feminist spirituality that tries to occupy the center of Christianity. As such it will be a help to both women and men.

Carmody, John. *Ecology and Religion.* Mahwah, NJ: Paulist, 1983. Another book that explores the new theology which the ecological crisis demands.

———. *Maturing a Christian Conscience.* Nashville, TN: The Upper Room, 1985. With his usual depth and style the author develops the idea of Christian ethics as personal spirituality.

Conn, Walter. *Christian Conversion: A Developmental Interpretation of Autonomy and Surrender.* Mahwah, NJ: Paulist, 1986. A masterly scholarly study which brings together developmental psychology and the philosophical and theological insights of Bernard Lonergan.

Gaventa, Beverly Roberts. *From Darkness to Light: Aspects of Conversion in the New Testament.* Philadelphia, Fortress, 1986. An illuminating study of the meaning of conversion in the New Testament.

Haughton, Rosemary. *The Passionate God.* London: Darton, Longman & Todd, 1981. A profound and deeply moving development of the theory of exchange of love between God and human beings.

Hillesum, Etty. *An Interrupted Life: The Diaries of Etty Hillesum 1941–43.* New York: Washington Square Press, 1985. One of the finest testaments to the triumph of love over fear and hatred I have read.

Jones, Alan. *Passion for Pilgrimage.* San Francisco: Harper & Row, 1989. Well written, moving meditations for the Lenten season.

Macmurray, John. *The Self As Agent* and *Persons in Relation.* London: Faber and Faber, 1957 and 1961. The Gifford Lectures of 1953–54. A profound analysis of the problem of the personal in philosophy. Difficult and dense reading, but well worth the trouble.

———. *Freedom in the Modern World.* London: Faber & Faber, 1968. A profound and prescient analysis of the dilemma of the modern world, originally given as radio lectures in 1930.

May, Gerald G. *Addiction and Grace.* San Francisco: Harper & Row, 1988. Another significant contribution to modern spirituality by a man who combines a profound grasp of psychology and the spiritual life.

Moore, Sebastian. *Jesus the Liberator of Desire.* New York: Crossroad, 1989. The brilliant sequel to *Let This Mind Be in You* in which Moore once again explores the meaning of the death and resurrection of Jesus for our lives.

Reiser, William, E. *Drawn to the Divine: A Spirituality of Revelation.* Notre Dame, IN: Ave Maria Press, 1987.

Speaks of the experience of God in our ordinary lives in an engaging, down-to-earth way.

Richards, Mary Caroline. *Centering in Pottery, Poetry, and the Person.* 2nd. ed. Middletown, CT: Wesleyan University Press, 1989. A very rich, poetic book. Centering, it seems to me, is a process of conversion.